W9-DBJ-744

Climbing: From Gym to Rock

Nate Fitch and Ron Funderburke

FALCON GUIDES

GUILFORD, CONNECTICUT
HELENA, MONTANA

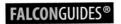

An imprint of Rowman & Littlefield

Falcon, FalconGuides, Outfit Your Mind, and How to Climb are registered trademarks of Rowman & Littlefield.

Distributed by NATIONAL BOOK NETWORK

Photos on the following pages are courtesy of Anthony D'Ercole: 43 (bottom left), 49 (middle and bottom), 67 (top), 110, 111, 123 (top), 124, 127, 135.

British Library Cataloguing in Publication Information available

Library of Congress Cataloging-in-Publication Data

Fitch, Nate.
  Climbing : from gym to rock / Nate Fitch and Ron Funderburke.
     pages cm
  "Distributed by NATIONAL BOOK NETWORK"—T.p. verso.
  ISBN 978-1-4930-0982-4 (paperback) — ISBN 978-1-4930-1505-4 (ebook) 1. Rock climbing—Handbooks, manuals, etc.
I. Funderburke, Ron. II. Title.
  GV200.2.F545 2015
  796.522'3—dc23

                                                    2015017362

∞™ The paper used in this publication meets the minimum requirements of American National Standard for Information Sciences—Permanence of Paper for Printed Library Materials, ANSI/NISO Z39.48-1992.

Contents

Introduction

When the first artificial climbing structures sprang into the general climbing consciousness, American rock climbers had already scaled the tallest cliffs in Yosemite Valley. They had already breached extreme 5.14 difficulties. Professional athletes, climbing instructors, and guides had already been earning their incomes on the cliffs and crags of the United States for the better part of the last century and into the current one. But, it was the CBS broadcast of the 1988 World Cup Climbing Championships at Snowbird, Utah, that catapulted American rock climbing into the mainstream. That broadcast inaugurated the era of the indoor climbing gym.

Artificial climbing structures have accelerated the popularity of rock climbing because they provide both beginner and world-class difficulties to any participant, in any location, and they can be used at any time of year. Today there are commercial climbing facilities in almost every major metropolitan area in the United States. In addition to commercial facilities, artificial climbing structures can be found at universities, high schools, and even elementary schools. There is at least one public or municipal climbing facility in every state and in most large cities. Atlanta, Georgia, for example,

The Climbing Wall Association estimates there are about 340 commercial facilities in the United States. It is further estimated that there are 50 to 100 users per 10,000 square feet at the typical commercial climbing facility.

can boast twelve public climbing facilities within its metropolitan area. American climbing has crept into the farthest reaches of the continent. A climber in Miami, for example, lives more than nine hours' from the nearest crag, one of the greatest distances between an indoor facility and a cliff top in the United States. The accessibility of indoor climbing facilities throughout the country has had a result that should be easy to anticipate: Rock climbing is more popular than it ever has been in the United States. On any given afternoon, anywhere in the country, Americans of every age, race, color, and creed are enjoying and learning the sport in unprecedented numbers.

What does this proliferation of indoor climbing mean to an American climbing culture that has historically been characterized by outdoor climbing? How has indoor climbing changed our community?

For one thing, our culture is unquestionably more diverse. Climbing is a sport now enjoyed by conformists and nonconformists alike, by the affluent and the indigent, the adventurous and the cautious. Our community acquires a louder voice as its ranks continue to swell, and the size of the climbing community naturally results in organizations that collate our interests. Organizations like the American Alpine Club, the Access Fund, the American Mountain Guides Association, the Climbing Wall Association, USA Climbing, and local climbing coalitions and clubs in every region of the country are all thriving.

Today, climbers tend to specialize in a particular aspect of the sport in a way that a World Wars era mountaineer could never have imagined. Some climbers prefer to stay in the gym. Some complement their indoor experiences with outdoor experiences. Some climb unroped on boulders exclusively, while some climbers lead climb and others do not. People climb in different subdisciplines for a wide variety of reasons: They enjoy challenges, new experiences, varying degrees of risk, being part of a community, outdoor environments, a nighttime indoor climbing session, and more.

A growing population with diverse and specialized interests instigates the same kind of growing pains

> More than 1,400 indoor climbing gyms exist in North America, serving an estimated 4,300 climbers each day. Predictably, a significant portion of those indoor climbers eventually participate in outdoor climbing as well; a 2012 study showed 27 percent of outdoor climbers were new to the sport.—Access Fund's ROCK Project

in the climbing community as it would in any other group. Every participant in the climbing community has a slightly different interest in the sport than the next participant. Every participant has slightly more or less experience and expertise than the next. Climbers are alternately more or less familiar with new settings and skills. But, despite all these differences, every participant also has a deep and abiding love of rock climbing. That is the common bond all climbers share, regardless of their skills, interests, political notions, or philosophy.

This text is ultimately meant to serve as a tool to give all indoor climbers a fair estimation of the skills they can expect to hone and develop so that they can begin to make a responsible and well-informed transition to an outdoor community. In doing so, we hope to help soothe many of the growing pains the climbing community feels when so many different users come together at a given outdoor venue. It is often inappropriate to apply the tools and techniques of an outdoor climbing venue to an indoor venue. In much the same manner, it is often inappropriate to apply an indoor norm to an outdoor setting.

In the following chapters, we hope to inventory all the differences that the average indoor climber can anticipate between an indoor setting and an outdoor setting. We hope to summarize the best practices when making a transition from one setting to the other. And, lastly, we hope to demonstrate that all climbers can have a reciprocal appreciation for the modern diversity of American climbing.

As a cautionary tale, it is not hard to imagine what will happen to the American climbing tradition if we do not find a way to gracefully transition between contexts and environments. We will slowly destroy and

corrode the places that inspire us as well as the sport we love.

This text cannot be read outside of the collaborative effort of groups like the Access Fund, the American Alpine Club, and the American Mountain Guides Association. The collective advocacy of the climbing community is harnessed by groups that are well organized and well funded. Throughout this text, we will refer to and rely upon the fact-finding, the education, and the science that these organizations have provided. It is hoped that the text will be a valuable resource to those looking to transition outside or those who have already begun this process. Using this resource under the aid of a qualified mentor or with professional instruction is a prudent path.

We encourage all readers of this text and all climbers in general to be well-informed, conscientious, and compassionate members of the climbing community, in all its manifestations. It is, after all, hard to imagine a world without rock climbing.

Imagine what it would be like to lose access to places like Smith Rock, Oregon. A heartbreaking thought!

An AMGA-certified climbing wall instructor (CWI) at work.

CHAPTER 1

Personal Responsibility

From the moment climbers enter an indoor climbing gym, their basic human needs have been accounted for. There is shelter from the weather, there is potable water available, snacks and nourishment are almost always offered for purchase, and all other bodily needs usually can be satisfied by a short drive or phone call. Necessary equipment is present for rental or purchase. Instruction is readily available. None of this is true about climbing outdoors. Most of America's rocks are located significant distances from towns, hospitals, and flushing toilets. They are, to put it simplistically, outside.

All climbers who venture outside, therefore, need a set of "outside" skills. In other outdoor sports, like hunting and fishing, mountain biking, or whitewater pursuits, these outside skills are an inextricable part of the sport, and there is no indoor equivalent. So, most participants in those sports learn to be competent and diligent outdoorsmen and outdoorswomen before they ever venture into the mountains, hills, woods, water, or wilderness. They know their success depends on it!

However, because climbing does have an indoor equivalent, a place where those outside skills are not necessary, learning to be outside involves its own learning curve. Additionally, there are cultural norms and etiquette to learn, new vocabulary and movement styles, and a host of novel technical skills.

As climbers, we all understand, intrinsically, that no power but our own can accomplish a great climb or overcome a boulder problem. We accept and relish the dearth of easy ways out, and the satisfaction that we feel upon completing a climb. All climbers eventually discover the limitless freedom that results from pursuing new challenges and accomplishing new objectives. In a similar way, there is no power on the planet that can more effectively take responsibility for an individual than an individual. When an individual sets his or her mind to know or do something, he or she will know it and will do it. We want to encourage and support this process.

Such a mind-set is a prerequisite to making a successful transition to outdoor climbing. Participants must be prepared to inventory all that they know and understand, forecast the things that they do not know and do not understand, and set themselves on a path to fill in the gaps. That is what "personal responsibility" means. Individual climbers must understand and accept that no one is going to rush to their aid, there are no easy ways out, and the fate of their outing, their health and safety, and the sustainability of the entire sport is entirely of their own making.

If a climber is willing accept this level of responsibility, then learning to climb outdoors can be tackled one skill set at a time. It can be a satisfying and a relatively safe endeavor. But, without it, climbers will drag themselves and their respective communities into peril, injury, environmental damage, loss of climbing resources, and more.

Personal Responsibility Self-Assessment

When trying to decide whether a certain trip or activity is appropriate, go through the following climbing self-assessment. You are ready to take personal responsibility if the answer is a definitive and unqualified "yes." If the answer is "no" or "sort of" or "maybe," it is probably a good idea to do more research, take a class, seek a mentor, or hire an instructor certified by the American Mountain Guides Association (AMGA).

Risk Management: Can I list all the risks that are specific to the venue, and do I have a tool or technique to manage all of those risks?

Environment: Do I know what kind of cliff I'm going to? Who owns it? Who manages it? Do I already know what climbs I want to do? How do I utilize those climbs?

Sustainability: Do I know how to apply all seven Leave No Trace (LNT) principles to this location?

Movement: Do I know the rock type and the most common moves at this location? Have I ever done those kinds of moves before on that kind of rock?

Culture: Can I name a few other kinds of climbers who I will likely see and meet there?

Equipment: When I get there, will I have more or less equipment than everyone else? Or will my kit be pretty much the same as everyone else's?

Belaying: How do people belay at this location? Have I ever done that before?

Rappelling: Do I need to rappel at this location? Have I ever done that before?

Anchors: What are the anchor setups for the climbs I want to do? Have I ever built anchors like that before?

Emergencies: If there is an accident, do I know what to do?

CHAPTER 2

Cliff Sustainability and Responsible Use

One of the first things a climber will need to appreciate about an outdoor environment is that climbers can have a measurable and destructive impact on the natural environment if they do not behave

A busy crag and the resulting impacts.

thoughtfully, conscientiously, and skillfully. Most noticeably, climbers have an opportunity to behave in a manner that sustains the resource not only for their own use but also for future generations. There are a few dominant themes as to the impact climbers can have on the natural environment and a corresponding set of best practices. They all start with being prepared in advance and researching the venue. It is important to be familiar with various rules, complexities, and issues before an outing. There are numerous sources for this research: a mentor, a climbing professional who works in the area or at the site, a guidebook (print or online), a ranger or land manager.

In this chapter, we will explore the impact climbers have on terrain features like the rock itself, ground

The member-driven Leave No Trace (LNT) Center for Outdoor Ethics teaches people how to enjoy the outdoors responsibly. The group has identified seven principles to help people make good choices for the environment and sustainability:

1. Plan ahead and prepare.
2. Travel and camp on durable surfaces.
3. Dispose of waste properly.
4. Leave what you find.
5. Minimize campfire impacts.
6. Respect wildlife.
7. Be considerate of other visitors.

This copyrighted information has been reprinted with permission from the Leave No Trace Center for Outdoor Ethics (LNT.org).

soil and other surfaces, and the air. We will discuss the impact climbers have on flora and fauna. And, lastly, we will discuss the overall impact climbers have on natural aesthetics. In each impact category, we will also discuss techniques and strategies for mitigating, eliminating, or minimizing those impacts.

Impacts on the Terrain

Even the most thoughtful climbers make an impact on the climbs they climb. In time, handholds break off from repeated use, footholds become polished by the passage of thousands of climbing shoes, and chalk slowly fills the tiny creases and crystals that give the rock its signature texture. Much of these impacts are inevitable, but many of them can be decelerated if climbers take personal responsibility for each tiny fraction of impact they create.

For example, carefully cleaning off footwear (climbing shoes or approach shoes) before beginning a climb will keep an already abrasive shoe from becoming a scouring pad. What's more, footholds that are covered in sand, dirt, and mud are difficult to stick to, even if the hold has not been permanently eroded. Many climbers deploy a small carpet at the base of a climb for precisely this purpose. Please, wipe your feet before entering the sanctuary!

Do not overuse chalk, and brush off any extra when possible. Using other grip enhancers (such as pof or rosin) can be very problematic to the rock.

Some climbers try to alter (chip, glue, or drill) the rock in order to "fix" it. This is not acceptable. Let nature and the natural traffic of climbers do all the "fixing." Brushing and cleaning holds can also have

Do not leave tick marks on the rock.

an impact on the rock. Be careful when brushing and cleaning; softer rock types can be damaged by simple brushing with a nylon toothbrush.

At the base of a climb, climbers make the same kind of impact on the ground soil that any foot traffic would make in any activity. Think of a heavily

Watching for fragile features on a rock face or boulder will help keep the terrain intact. Many loose features have been indicated with a large X marking to warn climbers about pulling too hard on them.

used baseball or soccer pitch: The grass has been worn away in certain parts of the field, and the soil beneath the bald spots has been packed down and pressurized; plant life and fragile layers of peat and duff cannot survive dense soil and trampling of this kind. Every climber should take personal responsibility to keep his or her impact isolated to one small area near the base of a climb. Large groups of climbers visiting an area together or over time have a greater effect than they realize. Try to tread lightly, and if bouldering, pad lightly and smartly.

Once all the plant life in a given area has been killed, erosion will begin in earnest, and base sites become an uninhabitable area of devastation for plants and animals. Once heavy erosion has begun, it will quickly accelerate and completely alter the natural appearance of climbing area.

Impact at the base of a climb and attempts at mitigation.

Also, believe it or not, many climbers and unin-formed users actually intentionally damage, vandalize, and disturb the terrain. Most often, these relatively small actions seem harmless, but in aggregate, they can grossly impact a cliff. Graffiti (either painted, carved, or etched in the stone) is unsightly and unnatural. Even worse is when individuals add graffiti to ancient rock art and carvings. These historical artifacts should be respected, not revised. Relocating large boulders (perhaps to create a seat or a table top) uproots animal habitat, accelerates the erosion of the surrounding soil, and often only serves a nominal purpose. Souvenir collecting of large boulders or stones is unfortunately common; while these rocks and boulders may look excellent in a flower garden, they look much better at the crag—where they belong.

If the impact of erosion, heavily chalked holds, vandalism, and other disturbances to terrain cannot be

Impactful graffiti.

abetted by conscientious use, the only other definitive solution to these problems is a long-term closure of land to all human use. In time, nature proves to be astoundingly recuperative, and all human damages eventually get washed or worn away. However, it would be more fun for everyone if such conservation efforts did not deprive climbers of the places they love so well. Mindful conservation of the landscape and terrain is an absolute priority for all users.

Impacts to Flora and Fauna

The presence of a big destructive mammal, like a human being, has a dramatic effect on any ecosystem. We have already discussed how foot traffic can destroy flora underfoot, and much of that kind of destruction cannot be avoided; it can only be consolidated and contained. But many climbers take further unnecessary steps, uprooting plants they dislike, such as thorny or poisonous plants, cactuses, scrub trees, or moss hummocks. Climbers should learn to work around such plant species instead of destroying them. In time, nature proves to be remarkably resilient; plants will learn to work around humans in exactly the same fashion. But that requires patience.

Animal life suffers mightily at the hands of rock climbers. Birds, bats, reptiles, rodents, and all sorts of creatures live in the cracks and fissures on a cliff, and these creatures should be left alone. Closures for nesting birds, rare plants, or other flora and fauna should be respected.

Remember that particularly dangerous animals, in the same manner as those thorny and poisonous plants, are no less entitled to prosper than their cuter counterparts. Poisonous snakes, stinging insects, biting animals, and large predators will learn to avoid humans just as the other species will, if we don't interrupt their natural process of adaptation.

Human refuse and food waste is probably one of the biggest unanticipated impacts that climbers make on animal life. All sorts of small creatures learn to populate a climbing area because there is a steady food source available to them. Predators in turn seek those creatures, and an entire food chain can be distorted by one seemingly harmless pistachio shell or orange peel. All food waste—apple cores, banana peels, even the smallest crumb or biodegradable morsel—should be packed out of the crag and disposed of properly. Pack out all your trash, including climbing tape!

Impact of Natural Aesthetics

Every climber does not need to admire nature with the same ardor as John Muir or Henry David Thoreau.

Cultural and historical resources.

But every climber does need to respect users who have and cherish that level of admiration. To this end, along with minimizing impact, there are a few gestures that every climber can make to sanctify the natural space of an outdoor crag.

Dispose of Human Wastes Properly

Human feces, urine, and other bodily fluids are offensive to see, smell, and touch. Not only are these materials offensive, they can be unsanitary and bio-logically dangerous. They should be regarded in the same manner as all other human wastes and removed from a crag.

Today, climbing areas are so popular that the age-old practice of digging small holes to bury human wastes is inappropriate. Many areas have seen those hastily dug holes excavated by subsequent users, pets, or other animals. A climber should consider how

An example of human-waste disposal kit.

several dozen users creating several dozen holes every-day will eventually saturate a pristine environment with holes, feces, and toilet paper. In time, climbers have to go farther and farther back into the woods to find an unused place, and all the cycles of plant and terrain destruction expand and perpetuate themselves. For urine, a common "pee trail" to an appropriate spot is usually an acceptable practice, provided everyone agrees, as a community, to use it. In any case, toilet paper, sanitary napkins, and all other waste-related products should be packed away from the cliff in the same fashion as excrement. Depending on your environment, there may be a preferred micro terrain to pee on, like a rock or pine needles. For feces, using a human-waste disposal kit that stabilizes the waste and allows removal is a best practice.

Use Established Trails

Creating new trails for simple shortcuts, bathroom excursions, or any other purpose is not an acceptable practice. New trails create terrain and flora-and-fauna impacts, and therefore building them is usually the collaborative prerogative of the climbing community and the land manager. Remember, a trail is a permanent and irremovable addition to a natural space. Individual users are not qualified to make such changes without the consensus of the land manager and the community. Do not block a trail with your stuff; not only is this bad form but it may encourage the creation of a new trail around you. There should only be one trail from point A to point B.

Control Pets

Pets are often an awkward and inappropriate addition to a cliff site. A domesticated animal is not part of the natural setting of the cliff. Unless a pet behaves as thoughtfully, conscientiously, and skillfully as its human owner, it will probably be a bad idea to bring most pets to the cliffs. Preservation of the natural environment is a personal responsibility that should be just as important to a climber as the health and happiness of a pet. If a pet can be taught to behave as well as a human, please leash and monitor them closely. Even well-behaved pets aggravate the poorly behaved ones.

Control Noise Pollution

The human voice is as much a part of nature as the call of a loon or the howling of a coyote. Be mindful of the collective power of human voices when sharing a crag with others. Yodeling might be a pastime left to Swiss pastures rather than American cliffs, especially if other users would rather listen to birds chirping. Likewise, music players, musical instruments, or voices in song can be splendid contributions to an individual experience, but they may be a great nuisance to other users. Climbers should be mindful and respectful with music and cellphones. Believe it or not, nature has its own playlist, and it can be quite remarkable.

Obey the Rules and Dictates of the Land Manager

Land managers often close cliffs or climbs, or instill other protocols and procedures aimed at the conservation and preservation of a natural resource. The reasons and justifications for those rules may not always be apparent and can be complicated. But, make no mistake, a land manager understands the biological, historical, and cultural significance of a cliff. That's their job. While we might not always agree with their strategies, all users must appreciate that the motives of the land manager and the climber are the same: to preserve the cliff for posterity. Accordingly, climbers should trust a land manager's wisdom or seek appropriate channels to complement their wisdom; defiance is usually not an appropriate way to do so. The rules regarding user fees, parking fees, camping, and permits should be followed. Trying to skip out on fees for a climbing site is not a way to represent climbers and foster continued use of a climbing resource.

Climber–Specific Actions

Climbers can act in many ways when at a climbing site, and these actions have effects on sustainability. For example, equipment can be consolidated and placed on a durable surface; no need to crush vegetation or force others to detour around it. Climbers can also be aware of historical trends that can limit access. The Access Fund, a national organization that works with sustainability and resource management, identified the following as common climber pitfalls that jeopardize access to outdoor climbing areas:

- Disrespecting the environment
- Overcrowding
- Accidents
- Disrespecting the landowner
- Not respecting closures
- Bolting inappropriately
- Failing to organize

Responsible Use by Managing Risk

Managing risk and ensuring a degree of safety is an important concept to connect with responsible use. A lack of risk assessment and management can lead to accidents. Accidents can lead to injury or death and sadden the climbing community. Unmanaged risk and accidents can impact the experience of others at the venue. Accidents, depending on their nature and your ability to manage a situation, may compel others to assume risk in order to aid in a rescue. Accidents and unmanaged risk have many impacts and can also jeopardize access to climbing areas.

CHAPTER 3

Land Management and Climber Advocacy

When climbing indoors, both the ownership and the management of the facility, and the rules that govern behavior there are known. This information is usually clearly posted on the wall, as part of a facility orientation liability release, and/or in a user agreement.

Outdoors, this information is also available, but it is often less obvious and requires more initiative from the user. In this chapter, we will explore who owns the crags and cliffs that climbers want to climb. We will discuss each of the major land-management agencies in the United States and how they operate. Lastly, we will give some guidelines for discovering what the rules and expectations are for a given climbing area.

Who Owns This Crag?

In the United States, climbing areas are owned and managed by federal, state, municipal, and private owners. In each case, a climber needs to demonstrate personal responsibility by understanding what governing body owns a climbing area, who the representatives and leadership of that body are, and which individuals handle the enforcement of each agencies policies and protocols.

Federal Agencies

Federal agencies include the following:

- The United States Forest Service, which is part of US Department of Agriculture

- The National Park Service, which is part of the US Department of the Interior

- The Bureau of Land Management, which is also part of the US Department of the Interior

Each organization is staffed and administrated differently, but all three are massive, multitiered bureaucracies that often seem remote and unaffiliated with an individual user. This, however, is not the case. When politicians appoint secretaries to our nation's executive departments, the behaviors of a single rock climber at a single crag are not, understandably, their chief concern. But, at each level of appointment, policy, and budget allocation, there are real-time consequences for rock climbers, which reminds each user to remember his or her duties of citizenship. Voting, participating in

Here are some examples of climbing areas found in federal management agencies:

- National Park Service: Yosemite National Park, California

- Bureau of Land Management: Red Rock Canyon National Conservation Area, Nevada

- US Forest Service: Rumney Rocks Day Use Area (White Mountain National Forest), New Hampshire

- National Monument: Devils Tower, Wyoming

the democratic republic, and advocating one's values and beliefs through petition, demonstration, and financial support are vital civic duties for rock climbers, just as much as for the next citizen. Such responsibilities are particularly vital for those users who rely on the US Forest Service, the National Park Service, and the Bureau of Land Management to sustain, enable, and regulate or deregulate our cherished sport.

State and Municipal Agencies

State and municipal agencies vary according to each body's (state or municipality) leadership, values, and users. A rock climber should feel a similar civic obligation in relation to these groups, but the size of the bureaucracy is obviously a much more impactful reality. At a municipal level, administrators can be swayed with a well-orchestrated advocacy or fund-raising campaign. At a state level, the immediate impact of climber advocacy and participation can also have real-time effects. Smaller bureaucracies are more quickly influenced by a vocal and organized user group, and

Here are some examples of climbing areas located in state or local management agencies:

- State park: The Needles, Custer State Park, South Dakota

- State park: Pilot Mountain State Park, North Carolina

- Municipality: Moss Island, Town of Little Falls, New York; Garden of the Gods Visitor and Nature Center, Town of Colorado Springs, Colorado

each climber's participation is even more vital in their local and regional communities.

Private Owners

Thousands of climbing destinations in the United States are owned by private landowners. These landowners may or may not relish the role of being a land manager. Some landowners assent to use of their property. Perhaps they value the sport and recreation, or perhaps small groups of climbers make a relatively small impact on the landowner's life (the landowner could personally know each user) or he or she does not feel burdened by legal or financial liability (this burden can change from state to state).

When the size of the user group increases, the landowner, like it or not, faces the prospect of becoming a land manager, and that is a time-, energy-, money-, and resource-intensive responsibility. Understandably, many landowners don't have the resources or the desire to take on obligations of that magnitude. They may resent the impact and destruction wrought by large groups and are reluctant to burden themselves with legal and financial liabilities. As a result, every climber should accept the undisputed reality that climbing on private property without the consent of the landowner not only demonstrates a lack of personal responsibility, but it is also a crime. Trespassing can result in some pretty stiff fines or imprisonment, and that will take a bigger toll on one's climbing career.

Many landowners, on the other hand, have accepted the responsibility of also being a land manager. The landowner and manager understand that in most states, recreational use statutes insulate them from legal and financial liability. They work alongside

Here are some examples of private climbing areas:

- Horseshoe Canyon Ranch, Jasper, Arkansas
- Horse Pens 40, Steele, Alabama

climbers and local climbing-advocacy groups and coalitions to maintain trails, toilet facilities, parking, and hardware at the crag. It is important for every climber to understand that the landowner and manager are not legally or ethically bound to any of these gestures or consolations. As result, every climber should feel a measure of gratitude and deference to these enormously generous landowners and managers. Climbers can demonstrate their gratitude and deference by abiding by any rules and expectations; making donations of time, money, and labor to the resource; and fostering personal relationships with the property owners.

Compliance

Regardless of the ownership or management of a given cliff, every climber should feel an obligation to comply with all rules, regulations, and policies. Many climbers delight in a countercultural, antiauthoritarian, and roguish outlook toward cultural norms, law enforcement, and any form of regulation in general. Much of American climbing was forged by this aversion to authority. But today, noncompliance, more often than not, does not reform an administration or change the rules, as it might have during a revolutionary era. This behavior usually results in the closures of the places that all climbers love.

Joshua Tree National Park
Rock Climbing and Bouldering

Find, read, and comply with local rules and regulations.

Within the confines of every land manager's expectations and policies, there is room for individual expression and creativity. Even if one land manager is particularly draconian or restrictive, there are other venues where management is less so. In the United States, there is something for every American rock climber. Wherever we climb, within whatever land-management entity, compliance with rules and regulations is just another way that we demonstrate personal responsibility.

Advocacy and Climbing Organizations

If compliance is one aspect personal responsibility, so is participation in far-reaching efforts toward advocacy, conservation, and climber access. Climbers, while compliant, cannot passively hope that administrative powers will prioritize their interests. It's pretty naive to think that all other Americans, besides rock climbers, aren't as self-interested as we are. As a result, climbers have a collective bargaining power, voice, and authority that is much more influential than an individual act of defiance. Every climber who wishes to join an outdoor rock climbing community should also feel compelled to join the organizations that work, lobby, raise funds, and advocate for our rights to use public lands in a sustainable way. Our collective existence depends on it.

National Organizations

National climber-advocacy groups are a logical way to combine our voices into something that large land-managing bureaucracies are more likely to listen to. Large groups have the power to accumulate large fund-raising efforts, to convene other large interest groups in a united effort, and to disseminate information quickly to all climbers. Every climber can find an organization that best speaks to their values; better yet, participate in and support all of them.

THE ACCESS FUND

www.accessfund.org

The Access Fund is one of the main national advocacy organizations that keep US climbing areas open. They campaign against overly restrictive management policies. They help purchase crags and climbing venues or maintain leases on properties to guarantee climber access. They organize conservation and sustainability campaigns through trail building and maintenance, cleanups, consultation, and countless other efforts. Founded in 1991, the Access Fund supports and represents over 2.3 million climbers nationwide in all forms of climbing: rock, ice, mountaineering, and bouldering. There are six core programs the Access Fund uses to support its mission on national and local levels:

- Climbing management policy (directed toward land managers)
- Local support and mobilization (helping smaller coalitions and groups get organized)
- Stewardship and conservation
- Land acquisition and protection
- Risk management and landowner support
- Education

Believe it or not, American climbing, in many of the places we find so unforgettable, would have been extinguished or outlawed without the efforts of the Access Fund. Their great work is ongoing in every facet of the sport.

THE AMERICAN ALPINE CLUB

www.americanalpineclub.org

Since 1902, visionary climbers and conservationists like John Muir understood that a collective voice would be the only way for climbers to effectively advocate their interests and the climbing landscapes. That's what the American Alpine Club (AAC) does and has always done. Many of their conservation and educational aims overlap and are coordinated with the Access Fund and the American Mountain Guides Association, but the AAC takes a huge stride forward in its service of its membership. AAC members gain access to a cornucopia of climbing-related information and resources in AAC publications like the *American Alpine Journal* (an archive of historic climbs and campaigns in every major mountain range) and *Accidents in North American Mountaineering* (an annual compendium of cautionary

---

Mission: To support our shared passion for climbing and respect for the places we climb.

Vision: A united community of competent climbers and healthy climbing landscapes.

Audience: Everyone who loves climbing.

Core Values:

- Authoritative climbing information, knowledge, and resources benefit and inspire us and future generations.

- Advocacy and leadership advance our climbing interests and promote conservation.

- Community and competency strengthen and embolden us to push our limits.

---

tales that every climber can learn from). The AAC has a library service and pools membership dollars to provide accident and rescue insurance to all its members, maintains accommodations and campgrounds for members in a handful of major climbing destinations, and is regionally organized to congregate members for social outings and climbing excursions. The American Alpine Club is best summarized by its mission, its vision, its audience, and its core values (see page 26):

THE AMERICAN MOUNTAIN GUIDES ASSOCIATION

www.amga.com

The American Mountain Guides Association (AMGA) ostensibly serves the nation's professional guides, climbing instructors, and guide services. But its mission suggests a greater relevance to all climbers: "to inspire and support a culture of American mountain craft." All climbers are, in one way or another, beneficiaries of the AMGA mission. Many of the best practices advocated by the Access Fund or the American Alpine Club were innovated or perfected by AMGA education programs, and many climbers gain their formative experience by hiring an AMGA-certified guide or climbing instructor or by taking a course offered by an AMGA-accredited program. Most modern climbing books, instructional manuals, and public education programs are either written by, edited by, or reviewed by someone trained or certified by the AMGA.

Furthermore, when the AMGA lobbies landowners and managers for professional and commercial access to a climbing venue, the interests of every climber are implicit in that campaign. Many climbers perceive a professional as another mechanism of control, much like a land manager. But it is important to remember that guides are climbers, too. As much as they may wish to take a student to a cliff on their workday, they also wish to recreate on that cliff on their day off. Furthermore, guides are just one of the many ways climbers choose to experience rock climbing. Many guided parties use a professional service to learn the mountain craft that all climbers aspire to. Whether you hire an AMGA-certified guide or climbing instructor to teach you to climb, or you read a book written by AMGA certified guides (like this one), or you learn to climb from friends and peers who benefited from AMGA mentorship, all climbers in all pursuits are aligned with the AMGA mission in one way or another.

Regional and Local Organizations

Large national organizations like the Access Fund, the AAC, and the AMGA are dependent on smaller regional and local coalitions and climbing clubs that

---

There are guidelines to help you discover the rules and expectations for a given climbing area:

- Talk to land managers.

- Find printed rules (online or at onsite offices/personnel).

- Talk to local climbers (at cliffs, gyms, online).

- Consult with the Access Fund, AAC, AMGA, and regional and local organizations.

- Get a guidebook for the area.

intimately understand and organize their communities and regionally nuanced cultures. In addition to participating in a national organization, climbers should not forget their local organizations. When a local coalition calls on the climbers in that region to bend their backs to a common task, the benefits of doing so are immediate and consequential.

In the Red River Gorge of Kentucky, for example, the combined efforts of the Access Fund, private donors, and the Red River Gorge Climbers' Coalition (RRGCC) have secured thousands of acres of prime sandstone climbing for all posterity. Not only that, but through the help of the membership, the coalition will continue to maintain the trails, parking, and hardware on the cliffs; to pay the property taxes; and to maintain adequate insurance to protect the cliffs from predatory litigation or competing interests.

If every other cliff in Kentucky, every public and private resource, were stripped from climbers, they would still have the RRGCC's properties to enjoy. Thanks to the RRGCC's stewardship, their example, and their advocacy, that is unlikely to happen. But the RRGCC offers all climbers a vision of what can happen when climbers quit begging land managers for the right to climb and simply purchase the cliffs for their own use and their posterity.

CHAPTER 4

Types of Crags

America's cliffs are innumerable, and within all those cliffs and crags and mountains there is enormous variety. An experienced indoor climber who wishes to make a transition to outdoors will want to seek out a few main types of cliffs for their first adventures. In general, a climber's first indoor experience likely involved a combination of toproping and bouldering; those disciplines of climbing are also ideal for one's first outdoor experience. Eventually, many indoor climbers learn to lead climb, and eventually many outdoor climbers will become interested in that pursuit as well. For this text we will focus on single pitch crags (<30m) that allow climbers to have a fulfilling and enjoyable climbing outing without the ability to lead climb. Toprope climbing is the logical first step for a transition to outside.

In this chapter we will disclose all the different types of cliffs that a climber will find in the United States, and we will focus special attention on those cliffs that are best suited to toproping.

Top Access Crags

Most outdoor climbers have their first outdoor climbing experiences on cliffs of this kind. A top access cliff is characterized by either (1) a bluff or escarpment or (2) a jumble of massive house-size boulders.

In each case, a climbing team can easily hike to the top of the cliff, build an acceptable anchor, and lower a climbing rope to the ground. Then, from the base of the climb, climbers and belayers can inhabit a climbing space that is technically very similar to a climbing gym setting. But there will be some obvious difference between the gym and the crag, and all users need to recognize and research those differences when making preparations for a visit.

Top access toproping crags have three main variables: the approach, the anchors, and the base site.

The Approach

The way a cliff is accessed varies wildly from one location to the next. But there are a few discernible patterns that all cliffs have in common. First, the trail that leads from the parking lot to the climbing area is usually clearly marked, maintained, or designated. If not, there will at least be signs of previous foot traffic. If the cliff is a bluff or escarpment, approach trails can either access the cliff from above or from below. Crags that are not characterized by a bluff or escarpment, essentially massive boulders, are almost always approached from the bottom, and the access to the top can be quite steep and tricky. Climbers should understand at a glance the terrain classification they will use to access a cliff top and be especially careful with exposed approaches.

The Anchors

Anchors can vary wildly from one cliff to the next. At one cliff, climbers and land managers may have installed permanent anchors that can be safely accessed without exposing an anchor builder to a cliff's edge. Sometimes, there are permanent anchoring components available, but they can be difficult or dangerous

Rock Climbing Movement Classes and Difficulty Grades

1st class: Walking.

2nd class: Hiking, mostly on trails.

3rd class: Scrambling; steep terrain on or off trails; use of hands, ropes, or fixed lines may be needed.

4th class: Climbing with serious fall potential; pulling with hands is needed; ropes and protection systems are commonly used.

5th class: Technical rock climbing; falls are "ground falls" and will result in injury or death. Rock climbing equipment and technical systems are used to protect climbers, and rock climbing techniques with hands and feet are needed.

5th class difficulty ratings are clarified by the Yosemite Decimal System (YDS) in the United States.

YDS Difficulty Grades

5.0–5.4: Minimal difficulty; beginner level

5.4–5.7: Moderate difficulty; beginner/intermediate level

5.7–5.10: Advanced difficulty; experience needed

5.10–5.15: Expert difficulty; experience and specific training needed

Note: This scale can expand as more difficult climbs are completed.

Other Grades

Plus and minus signs (+/–) are given to routes to denote difficulty, for example, 5.9+ is more difficult than 5.9–.

Letter grades (a, b, c, or d) are sometimes added to a route that is a 5.10 or higher grade to indicate further difficulty, for example, 5.10a, 5.10b, 5.10c, 5.10d, 5.11a. 5.11b, and so on. The letter a indicates a lesser difficulty and d denotes the most difficulty.

Protection grades are given to indicate the ability to protect a climb when using traditional lead-climbing techniques.

G: Protection is good and frequent.

R: Protection is adequate, but significant sections of the climb may not have protection; there is potential for long falls and ledge/ground falls.

X: Protection is minimal, and long consequential falls are possible.

Commitment grades indicate how long a climb will take an experienced climbing team to complete.

Grade I: A climb requiring 1 to 2 hours

Grade II: 2 to 4 hours

Grade III: A climb that takes the better part of a day. For some parties, a Grade III could require all day.

Grade IV: A climb that takes all day.

Grade V: A climb that takes more than one day.

Grade VI: A multiday climb.

6th class: Minimally featured rock; using hands and feet to move is not possible. Equipment is used to hold the climber and aid progress on the rock—Aid Climbing.

Aid Climbing Grades—describe the frequency of secure equipment placements.

Natural anchors in use and misuse?

to access. At another crag, the use of trees and other natural features may predominate. Sometimes access to these natural features is quite exposed; at yet another area, the use of vegetation may be prohibited, and removable artificial protection may be required. In any case, climbers should understand what the prevailing anchoring tactic is for a giving cliff before they arrive. They should have adequate equipment to meet those challenges and be familiar with how to use that equipment effectively. Some of these skills will be covered later in this book.

The Base Site

Once a toprope has been established, the base site is where the team will effectively live and operate while using the climb. Typically climbers need to be strategic with how they organize their equipment, where they choose to belay, and how they share the cramped space with everyone else. Additionally, some base sites pose challenging terrain to the climbing rope and its users. Sandy cliffs, fire-damaged cliffs, muddy areas, and heavily vegetated areas all demand that climbers bring appropriate tools (like rope bags and mats), attire, and footwear to the cliff. Rocks and roots can cause tripping hazards or injury to a climber who falls close to the ground, despite a sound belay. Lastly, some base sites offer a plethora of ground anchoring options, like boulders and trees; others do not. Climbers need to be prepared to deal with places where ground anchors may or may not be available.

Bottomless Crags

Many crags do not have a base. They are essentially "bottomless." Climbers cannot approach to or leave from the bottom. Belaying at the bottom is not an option. These bottomless crags need to be top managed, and all climbers must return to the top via the rock face. This can present many challenges that require advanced techniques.

Lead Climbing Crags (Traditional or Sport)

Many crags have been designed and equipped for sport or traditional lead climbing. At such crags, toproping is still a routine occurrence, but, typically, it can only occur after a lead climber has led the route, established an anchor, and lowered to the ground. Additionally, someone in the climbing party, either by toproping or lead climbing, must retrieve the anchoring materials and lower or rappel back to the ground. Due to the common sequence of leading, toproping, and anchor retrieval, Lead climbing crags have permanent anchors. Those anchors vary wildly, but, in general, there is a fixed and permanent point from which a climbing party can rappel or lower. This text will not focus much of its attention to lead climbing crags, including multipitch crags. Utilizing crags of this nature makes the inexperienced user even more reliant on a mentor or climbing professional. Effectively functioning to climb at a lead climbing crag represents a serious step beyond top access toproping.

Multipitch Crags

Much like the lead climbing crag, outdoor rock climbers will see a much different set of climbing skills at work when they visit a multipitch crag. These crags are primarily characterized by their size: Tall looming faces take climbing parties much higher than half a standard rope length and any climbing gym in the world. Even an experienced indoor climber usually is ill-prepared to deal with climbs of that magnitude.

It is possible, and not uncommon, for climbing parties to use a multipitch crag in the same manner as a smaller lead climbing crag. In that scenario, the lead climber would simply lower from the top of the first pitch and the entire party could toprope that first pitch. There are some considerations:

- Is there a permanent anchor on top of the first pitch?

- What is the rope length required to toprope?
- Multipitch lead-climbing teams have the right of way.

Hybrid Crags

These crags could contain one or more of the above crag types: top access, base, lead climbing, top managed, top managed (bottomless), and multipitch. Approach these crags with caution as the terrain can change from climb to climb. Determine the type of crag for a particular climb, and function and manage risk as described above and in later chapters of this text.

CHAPTER 5

Movement

Rock climbing is one of the most counterintuitive ways to use a human body. Its most challenging aspect is the way the brain's natural instinct to shift the body's center of gravity from one foot to the other is short-circuited by objects in the hands, such as handholds.

An experienced indoor climber, thankfully, has already spent much of his or her climbing career unlearning this natural response. An experienced indoor climber will grab a handhold, distribute weight to his or her feet from a low step to a higher step, and redistribute that weight instantly as they grasp the next handhold. Most experienced climbers make this weight transfer and center of gravity shift unconsciously. This fundamental skill is the only thing climbers really need to be able to do in order to begin enjoying outdoor rock climbing; other outdoor-specific moves are probably best learned outdoors. In this chapter, we will explore some of the movement techniques that an indoor climber will need to begin to master as they explore the outdoor climbing realm. In this chapter, we will illustrate the slight tweaks to climbing technique that correspond with key outdoor-terrain features, like cracks and slabs.

Indoor Surfaces versus Outdoor Surfaces

Almost all indoor climbing surfaces are created by a flat plane of material, like plywood or textured polyurethane, from which climbing holds protrude. As a result, the climber's body also protrudes from the climbing surface. Outdoors, by contrast, the vast majority of climbing holds are created by a relief in the climbing plane, not a protrusion. So the climber's body does not protrude from the rock as much.

One of the most immediate and obvious consequences of this fundamental difference is that outdoor climbers can distribute more weight to their feet at all times because their hips are more easily aligned with their feet. An indoor climber who can adapt to this new reality can find a surplus of stamina for steep cruxes or sustained climbs, because those difficulties more closely mimic the indoor surface on which they

Holds created by a relief in the climbing plane (top) and protruding from the climbing plane (bottom).

learned to climb. By extension, an indoor climber who cannot perceive the wealth of footing they usually have available, and the opportunity to rest on that footing, will likely find outdoor climbing incredibly frustrating.

Footing

An indoor climber is quite adept at standing on a protrusion, and so they adapt their stances according to the size and position of those footholds. They have learned to use the power in a down-turned big toe to bear into the smallest and smoothest nubbins and to use the sharp outside edges of their shoes to curl into a backstep. These movement strategies will be crucial in an outdoor setting, too, but the terrain does not present itself in the same way. Outdoor climbers are not retraining their feet so much as they are retraining their eyes.

Imagine the following sequence: A climber is locked off with both hands on a strenuous match. They look down immediately to find their foothold for a high step. An indoor climber is searching for a certain color tape or a certain color hold or any protrusion from the surface they are climbing. Once spotted, an indoor climber instantly edges, smears, or backsteps according to the size and position of that hold. Outdoors, that indoor climber's eye must make a much different kind of search. More than likely, the foothold he or she is looking for will have been a previous handhold. It's pretty easy to spot therefore, as it will be chalked or at least the climber's hand will have touched it in the previous sequence. But sometimes that footing is not so obvious; sometimes the footing is not a previous handhold. The outdoor climber's eye must learn to

Footwork on a climbing plane relief: smearing and a foot in a pocket.

perceive any relief in the climbing plane as a potential foothold. That relief could be a pocket, smear, or edge of an arête. There will not be any special coloring or designation that indicates that this particular relief is the one a climber is looking for. An outdoor climber's eye learns to read the relief, shape, direction, and texture of the climbing surface—not the route color or markings. Experienced climbers do this while understanding the miniscule size of holds that feet can effectively utilize with modern climbing shoes and practice. Once all that information has been gathered, an outdoor climber must make choices. It's an engaging puzzle!

Opposition

Outdoor climbing is also characterized by converging and diverging planes, much more so than indoor climbing. Some climbing gyms have dihedral features (two converging planes), but many do not. Outdoors, on the other hand, it is hard to find a cliff that does not have a dihedral or corner system somewhere on the feature. Similarly, some climbing gyms have soaring arêtes (two diverging planes), but many do not.

Converging planes create a corner, and divergent planes create an arête.

Outdoors, however, an arête is one of the most common features at any crag.

In all these cases, a climber pushes or pulls against converging or diverging planes in order to stabilize in the opposing direction of those planes: opposition movement!

There are three kinds of opposition movement:

- **Pulling techniques:** lieback, undercling
- **Pushing techniques:** mantle, stemming
- **Squeezing techniques:** double sidepulls, heel and toe hooks

Pulling: Undercling—pull up with a hand (or hands), stabilize the pull with the feet.

Pulling: Lieback—pull out and back with the hands, stabilize the pull with the feet.

Squeezing: Sidepulls.

Pushing: Mantle.

Because these features are much more common outdoors, the techniques used to climb the corner and arête are signature techniques. These techniques are rarely found on a sustained feature indoors.

Pushing techniques, like a mantle or stemming corner, can be found on every basalt and granite crag in the world. In each case, the climber pushes with palms or fingertips in order to establish footing. In the case of stemming, the footing is on two converging planes. In most cases, especially when the angle between the two planes is more acute, the footing will consist of simple smears and outward pressure. When the angle between the two planes is more obtuse, a climber will need to rely more on the relief of the plane on each side, a delicate protrusion, or some other feature.

Squeezing techniques will commonly present when a climber can sidepull or heel/toe hook an entire feature of the rock like an arête. In the case of the arête, the plane of the rock diverges away from the climber. Sometimes, he or she climbs to the left of the divergence, sometimes to the right, given the availability of features on either side. In either case, the hold on one plane or the other avails the arête itself as a sidepull hook. As the climber transitions from one side of the arête to the other, the entire feature is squeezed between the climber's hands and feet, like a caliper or clamp would.

Cracks

The earliest American rock climbers had fewer mediums for their climbing than we do today. When they chose to lead, they first targeted a crack system or line of weakness that would accept their pitons, chocks,

Cracks! Given the size of the crack, the next major outdoor variation in technique involves the jam.

and other methods of protection. As a result, climbers learned to climb these kinds of features first and foremost. Today it is inconceivable for climbers of that era that an indoor climber can develop world-class climbing abilities without ever learning to climb a crack. While that is clearly a modern reality, an indoor climber who wishes to enjoy outdoor climbing will need to give those golden-era climbers some credit and learn the age-old craft of *crack climbing*.

Many cracks are climbed using the opposition movement techniques already mentioned. But many cracks are simply abrupt fissures in a plane of the climbing surface. The crack is the relief of the climbing plane. So the climber does not climb on a series of holds, but instead finds ways to wedge the body (or body parts) into the crack. This *straight-in* form of crack climbing has two main variations in its techniques. The first is most obviously based on the size of the feature; the smallest crack, accepting only the tips of a climber's fingers and the edges of his or her shoes, is a much different kind of climb than the widest cracks, ones that swallow the climber's entire body. In

Jams

- **Constriction jam:** Target a constriction in the crack and simply wedge the appropriate-size body part into the crack.

- **Compression jam:** Target a parallel crack and a body part is torqued, twisted, fattened, or squeezed to apply outward pressure to the two parallel surfaces.

Some constriction jams: fingers, feet, and hand.

each case, climbers must learn to use the appropriate body part for the crack size.

When cracks are really big—body-size chimneys—climbers use more of an opposition style of movement. Not only are the palms and feet good for pressing against the two opposing planes, but climbers might push the back and buttocks against one side of the chimney and both feet and hands on the opposite side, and then inch their way up the feature with small feet and butt scoots.

Some compression jams: fist, ring, hands, fingers, chicken wings, and stacks.

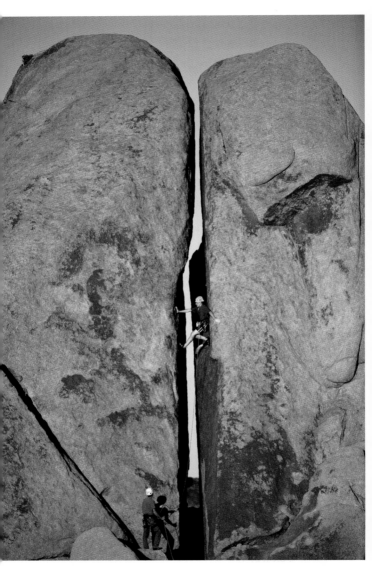

Chimney climbing!

Crack Climbing Tips

- Look for constrictions to jam, and be prepared to use compression jams.

- Look outside the crack for holds.

- Take rests only when absolutely needed—keep moving.

- Commit to movement and efficiency.

- Be creative!

Slabs

While some climbing gyms have long low-angled features (typically found in a beginner's area), the holds protruding from that low-angled plane make the climbing

Slab Climbing Tips

- Drop heels.

- Keep your hips out.

- Realize the true angle of the rock!

- The palms of your hands can act like feet: mantel and push down.

- Take rests only when absolutely needed—keep moving.

- Do not reach too high.

- Commit to movement and efficiency.

Climbers in action. A palm mantel and smearing.

quite rudimentary. Outdoors, however, low-angled planes have typically been worked smooth by weather and erosion. The lack of obvious holds characterizes this climbing medium. An outdoor climber must perceive that the low-angled nature of such a plane makes the entire plane a continuous hand- and foothold, irrespective of distinctive features. Climbers must learn to optimize friction with near-constant smearing and dynamic weight transfers between the slightest concavities.

Movement Practice

There are many ways to practice movement skills. Specific training, drills, or activities are beyond the scope of this text. However, you should try to be aware of

Practicing movement skills via bouldering.

your movement when toproping. What is working for you? What is not? Get feedback and help from your partner. An experienced mentor or climbing professional will be able help you with your movement skills. Ask more-experienced climbers about how they would climb a particular route. Be deliberate and conscious about the techniques or tips applied.

Many climbers enjoy bouldering (climbing on small rocks, relatively low to the ground and unroped) or traversing (climbing sideways, relatively low to the ground and unroped) as means to warm up for the day and to get used to the rock and how it climbs, as well as to practice their movement. Some choose this discipline for their primary pursuit of climbing. It's a challenging, unique, and often gymnastic movement that certainly has its appeals. You can also do lots of moves (of many varieties in the right area) in a short amount time!

CHAPTER 6

Equipment

Typically, a visit to the gym does not require much equipment. First-time visitors have access to everything they will need to use a climbing facility, as do more-experienced users who forget a piece of equipment. Outdoor climbers do not have this luxury. Outdoor climbers will need to select, maintain, and use all of their own equipment, and that requires a much greater degree of personal responsibility. A user needs not only to select and purchase equipment but also to understand each item's design, intended use, materials, strengths, weaknesses, and life span. In this chapter we will review how equipment is designed, manufactured, and reviewed or endorsed in the United States. We will explore the materials used to construct each item and how that ultimately guides a climber to maintain and care for their tools. Lastly, we

Equipment Best Practices

- Keep equipment organized and neat.

- Treat all equipment with respect—your life depends on it!

- Use all climbing equipment according to the manufacturer's specifications.

- Inspect equipment before use!

suggest the minimum array of equipment necessary to have a comfortable and satisfying climbing outing at a typical crag.

How Is It Made?

It is important to appreciate how all climbing equipment is designed and manufactured. The manufacturers of climbing equipment make concerted efforts to educate users about their products, what a product is designed to do, what it is not designed to do, how best to care for their products, and how often to replace them.

In the United States, the best way to discover how a piece of equipment is manufactured, what it is designed to do (what each feature is also designed to do), and the strengths and weaknesses of the equipment, is to consult the manufacturer. Every piece of climbing equipment is distributed with a small bulletin and informational document about the unit's manufacture date, its shelf life, the best practices, design specifications, composition, working load, and more. Much of this information is also printed, tagged, or stenciled on each item as a helpful reminder to the user.

A climber should read that document and understand everything it says. If not, ask! Manufacturers have made an art of answering consumer inquiries in a timely and effective manner.

There are also neutral and nonprofit third-party resources that climbers can refer to when researching equipment. The Union of International Alpine Associations (UIAA), for example, exists to educate climbers about the tools they use, the books they read, and the instructors they hire.

Examine Black Diamond's oval carabiner, for example. Everything Black Diamond prints on the unit, everything they print on the accompanying document, and everything the design team and manufacturers tell you about that carabiner is accurate and trustworthy.

But, if you wanted to know what a third-party organization thought of the unit, the UIAA is a great resource. A reader will discover (www.theuiaa.org) the standards to which all carabiners are tested in order to receive a UIAA certification, and an updated archive of each manufacturer's products. If a product has been tested and endorsed by the UIAA, a thorough consumer can discover when, how, and how often every product is reviewed.

The Conformité Européenne (CE) is a process and marking by the Euopean Commission (www.ec .europa.eu). This agency tests products and ensures they act and perform as the manufacturer promotes. This mark indicates the product follows applicable European Conformity directives and regulations.

What Is It Made Of?

Climbers can split all materials into two main functional categories: hard goods and soft goods. Hard goods are generally made of metal or plastic; they are load-bearing, critical-application tools like carabiners, belay devices, and removable protection. Soft goods are generally made of textiles for attachment tools like slings, harness, cords, or ropes.

Hard Goods

A climber's hard goods are generally made of metal (aluminum or steel) and plastic (organic polymer).

Critical components are usually made of some steel alloy. Housings or larger body parts are usually made of aluminum, and cosmetic or noncritical components are usually made of plastic. A climber can easily discover these properties and their behaviors to infer what to do with their tools, how to care for them, and when to retire them. All metal goods, for example, should not be used when they are visibly corroded, worn by wear and continued use, or damaged by misuse. All plastic goods should likewise be used within

Inspection Tips

- Use your tactile and visual senses.

- Be thorough.

- Utilize in-depth tactile and visual inspection to suspect areas as a second level of inspection.

- When in doubt, ask the manufacturer or contact a climbing professional.

A severely worn carabiner.

Hard Goods Inspection

Look for the following conditions:

- Corrosion
- Worn by wear and use
- Visible damage
- No longer function as designed
- Loose or missing parts
- Non-working

Hard Goods Care

- Store in a cool, dry, inert place, free from contaminants.
- Avoid dropping equipment onto hard surfaces; never throw it.
- Do not engrave.
- Lubricate per the manufacturer's recommendation.

Hard Goods Retirement

Dispose of equipment with any of the following conditions:

- Failed inspection
- Expired manufacturer's shelf life
- Dropped more than 10 feet onto a hard surface

When in doubt, retire it.

their recommended shelf lives (based on the decomposition rate of the organic materials).

Soft Goods

A climber's soft goods are generally made of polymers: nylon and any number of materials generically known as *ultra high molecular weight polyethylene* (UHMWP). Off the shelf, a manufacturer may have proprietary versions of UHMWP like Spectra, Dyneema, or Dynex. There are a few major differences between nylon and UHMWP that generally translate into two main application categories: Equipment composed of nylon is generally designed for dynamic applications, while equipment composed of a UHMWP is generally designed for a static application.

This application difference is important! We'll see some specific examples of these applications in Chapters 9 through 12.

Generally speaking, a climber simply needs to know that different polymer textiles are applied to

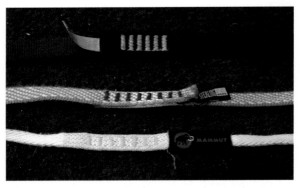

Slings are a commonly used soft good. They can be made of nylon, a blended hybrid, or UHMWP.

Nylon versus UHMWP

Nylon	UHMWP
Low cost	High cost
High stretch	Low stretch
Heavier per length	Greater strength-to-weight ratio
Low abrasion resistance	High abrasion resistance
Higher melting point	Can be slippery
Better sustains repeated flexing	Very high strength loss when knotted
Absorbs water	Hydrophobic

different equipment because of their load-bearing properties or their dynamism (dynamic force absorbing properties). Both materials need to be cared for similarly.

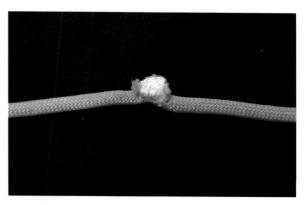

A failed soft-goods inspection: exposed core.

Soft Goods Inspection

Look for the following conditions:

- Worn by wear or use
- Visible damage: cuts, fraying, exposed core fibers, faded color, stiffness, bumps, flat spots, hourglass shapes, glazing, burns, crusty or crunchy spots, or any other irregularities

Soft Goods Care

- Store in a cool, dry, inert place, free from contaminants.
- Avoid ultraviolet (UV) degradation, mold and mildew, acids and bases.
- Don't expose to high heat or excessive friction.
- Avoid stepping on it.
- Protect it from sharp edges and abrasion.
- Leave it unknotted and coiled (organized) for the next use.
- Wash as needed as instructed by the manufacturer.

Soft Goods Retirement

Dispose of equipment with any of the following conditions

- Failed inspection
- Expired manufacturer's shelf life

When in doubt, retire it.

What Do I Need?

Unlike the climbing gym, equipment is not provided to users when they venture into the outdoors. So, every climber and every collective climbing team needs a standard selection of equipment. The following inventory is more than adequate to provide many enjoyable outings!

Apparel

All clothing appropriate for rock climbing has a few common traits all climbers will appreciate:

- Accommodates a wide range of motion
- Manages adverse weather conditions
- Durable

Shoes

Climbing shoes come in many shapes and sizes that an indoor climber may already be familiar with. Outdoor shoes typically have the following requirements:

- They are comfortable.
- They can be worn a long time.
- They smear and jam effectively.
- They excel on moderate terrain.
- They are durable for the rigors imposed by inexperienced outdoor climbers.

Chalk Bag

Indoor climbers enjoy and have become accustomed to the use of climbing chalk, and it is still a viable aid to the climber's grip in an outdoor setting as well. Outdoors, however, the holds cannot be removed and cleaned, so a sparing and conservative ethic should temper the climber's use of chalk. Tick marking, excessive chalk use, and spills create unsightly climbs, spoil route-finding challenges for others, and distort the natural appearance of a crag. Chalk lightly! Climbers can attach a chalk bag to their bodies in any number of ways (with webbing/cordage belt, carabiner, etc.).

Backpack

Because all outdoor crags involve a short hike from the parking area to the cliff, a backpack becomes essential gear for an outdoor climber. When selecting a backpack, look for models that are big enough (typically 35L to 45L) to hold all the climbing equipment needed inside and durable enough to withstand the abuses of a rock-climbing outing. Keeping equipment inside a pack prevents dangling items that are easily damaged, lost, or entangled in vegetation while hiking. Dangling items can also slam into you or others.

Helmet

A climbing helmet that is designed and endorsed for rock climbing is a crucial piece of equipment on outdoor climbing excursions. It has become more

Helmet types: rigid with an interior "spider" webbing suspension, hybrid (spider and bicycle), bicycle, and all foam.

Proper Helmet Fit: Protect Your Head!!

- Wear it parallel to the user's eyebrows and keep the forehead covered.

- It should evenly cover the front and back of the skull.

- A snug chinstrap should not irritate the ears or squeeze against the throat.

- It should move with your head and stay in place.

and more the norm for climbers to wear a helmet on and around the cliff. Look for a model that is UIAA approved for climbing, fits comfortably, and is durable.

Many climbers are averse to helmet use because they have never found a model that fits their head very well. Take the time to select and fit the climbing helmet so that is comfortable and inconspicuous during use—so it makes you want to wear it!

Harness

Much like a helmet, a climbing harness should be designed and approved for rock-climbing use. Utility harnesses, improvised seats, and industrial harnesses are inappropriate for recreational climbing outings. A UIAA- or CE-approved climbing harness, on the other hand, strikes the perfect balance between weight, comfort, and functionality.

There are few important things to keep in mind when selecting a harness for outdoor use: comfort, the need to carry equipment, layers of clothing

Harness Features

Number of buckles:

- Do I need to adjust the position of the gear loops to make them symmetrically oriented on my hips? This may be easier to do on your body with two buckles.

Types of buckle:

- Do I need a speed (autolocking) buckle? Am I the kind of person who forgets to double back? If yes, do not forget to tuck the tail!

- Do I need to double back my buckle? Do I have 3 or more inches of tail after the double back?

Number of gear loops:

- Do I need to carry a lot of equipment? Will I need to eventually?

Amount and location of padding:

- Do I hang in my harness a lot? More padding will be needed!

Adjustability:

- Do I change clothes a lot or use my harness in multiple seasons? You may need adjustable waist and leg loops.

underneath, and durability. Try on a few models to find the best fit. Be sure to experiment with different clothing layers when sizing a harness; if the harness

Proper harness fit.

will be worn outdoors with lots of clothing, be sure to size it accordingly. Find a model that sits comfortably above the hips and on the true waist, with leg loops that encircle the upper thigh at the crotch.

Dynamic Rope

At the gym, climbing ropes are conveniently provided for the user. These ropes may or may not have all the features, function, and durability needed for outdoor climbing.

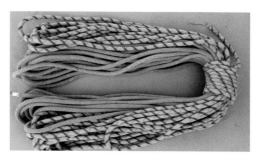

A bicolor dynamic single rope, ideal for outdoor toprope climbing.

Types of Dynamic Ropes

Single: A single rope common for toproping and single pitch lead climbing; the norm.

Half: Two ropes used in conjunction with each other in lead climbing applications; generally not clipped to each protection point together.

Twin: Two ropes used in conjunction with each other in lead climbing application; must be clipped to each protection point together.

The ideal first outdoor climbing rope is UIAA approved, designed and inspected for single-strand use; it is, in other words, a single rope. It should be durable and tough; 10mm or 10.5mm is usually a good diameter. A dry coating or treatment will also add a bit more resistance to sheath abrasion (and additional cost!). The climbing rope should have a middle mark that is easy to distinguish; a bi-color rope makes it easy to find the middle mark at any time. Lastly, the rope should be a dynamic single rope that can translate into lead climbing once a climber is ready to learn those skills.

Static Rope

These ropes are rare in the gym. They are characterized by a lower stretch (elongation) than a dynamic rope. A UIAA-approved static rope is a great tool at the crag. A static rope 9mm (or more) in diameter can be used for anchoring and protecting oneself while working at the top of a cliff.

Rope Properties

Elongation. Each rope is different!

- Static elongation (body weight loads applied): usually 4–8 percent of working length

- Dynamic elongation (lead fall loads): usually 20 percent or more in a lead fall

Impact force. This is the amount transmitted to a climber or anchor after elongation.

Rated number of falls. This is the number of severe lead falls a rope withstood during a UIAA 101 test before failure; in real world conditions ropes can hold many more typical lead falls.

Factor falls. Factor is calculated by dividing the lead fall length by the amount of rope in the system. Factor two falls are the highest theoretically possible result. (20 foot fall length on 10 feet of working rope length)

What does this all mean?

- Many of these statistics do not really apply to toproping.

- Watch sharp edges. Don't fall on them and don't allow a sharp edge to wear on the same spot of a rope. Ropes under tension can cut easily.

- As always, know your rope!!! Check with the manufacturer for specifics about your rope, and use it per the manufacturer's guidelines. Take good care of it!

- Have good technical skills and judgment. The strongest rope in the world will not be of assistance if it's connected to a bad anchor or used with poor decision-making.

- Rope inspection, care, and retirement. Follow the guidelines for soft goods. Your climbing rope is the single most important piece of gear you own.

Slings (aka Runners)

Slings are commonly used when constructing anchors, tethers, ground anchors, and more. While there are many styles and lengths available, the most useful slings for rock climbing are nylon, $9/16$ to $11/16$ inch (14–17mm) in width, and 24 inches (shoulder length) to 48 inches (double length) (60–120cm) in length. Quickdraws are a relatively short fixed length version of a runner. A runner is a sling with a carabiner on

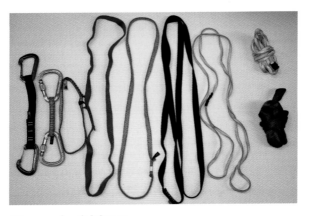

Slings and quickdraws.

each end. These are typically rigid and common in climbing gyms and many outdoor applications.

Accessory Cords

Nylon cords are also commonly used when constructing anchors, tethers, ground anchors, friction hitches, and more. Typically, friction hitches are smaller diameter cords, because the disparity between the hitch material diameter and the diameter of the thing it is tied around is advantageous. The greater this disparity, the greater the friction and gripping power. A 5mm accessory cord loop tied into an 8-inch diameter loop usually works quite well on any climbing rope diameters between 10mm and 10.5mm.

A longer length of cord is typically referred to as a cordellette and is used primarily for anchoring. Unlike 6mm nylon loops used for friction hitches, a single strand of cordellette is often a critical link (anchors, tethers, etc.). Cordellette should be wider and tougher;

Cordellette and accessory cord loops: 5.5mm UHWMP Titan cord, 6mm UHWMP Powercord, 6mm nylon, 7mm nylon.

7mm nylon cords measuring 16 to18 feet in length are usually perfect.

As always, know what your cord is made of, use it according to manufacturer's specs, and apply it wisely!

Carabiners

Carabiners are manufactured in a wide range of shapes and styles, and designed to serve a wide range of applications. For our purposes, carabiners have two main functions: critical link applications and noncritical link applications.

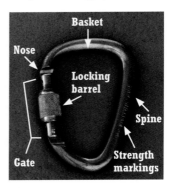

Parts of a carabiner: gate, locking barrel, spine, nose, basket, strength markings.

Critical links, such as the connection between a belay device and a harness, must not fail! These carabiners are not part of a

---

Carabiner Features

Size

Shape

Locking mechanism

Gate type, nose, and configuration

Information on spine

These features are only important in terms of application. Pick the features you need for the task!

Load in direction along the spine!

- NO cross loading
- NO triaxial (three-directional) loading
- NO open gate loading
- NO levering on rock

redundant system. Critical links should use a carabiner with some sort of locking mechanism to safeguard the connection from gate interference that could compromise the link. In general, the more secure a locking mechanism, the more time it takes to operate. For every locking mechanism, regardless of its security, continuous inspection and double checks are vital strategies in the appropriate use of a critical link. Carabiner shape, size, and locking-mechanism security should be considered for each application.

Noncritical links can be nonlocking as they are usually deployed as part of a redundant system, and failure has a low consequence for climber security. When used in pairs with gates opposite and opposed a pair of nonlocking carabiners has the effective security of a locking carabiner.

A close-up of the spine markings on a carabiner. Notice the strength (18kN) when loaded along the spine (as intended by the manufacturer).

Belay Devices

As with many of the tools already discussed, selecting a belay device presents an outdoor rock climber with enormous varieties to choose from. The biggest difference between an indoor and an outdoor setting is that many of the tool choices are made for the indoor user. The facility may require the use of a particular tool or only teach one belay tool in its classes. Outdoor climbers should be prepared to have two devices, and they should know how to use them both equally well. Every outdoor climber would be well-advised to purchase a tuber device and an assisted braking device (ABD).

Tuber/Aperture devices have a simple and classic design. Two rope slots make the device an excellent choice for belaying off the climber's waist or rappelling. An **ABD** is a more complex and expensive tool, but its applications in an improvised rescue (and

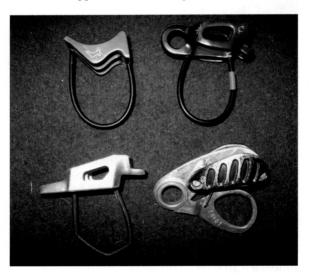

Tuber/Aperture belay devices.

others) are incomparable in terms of efficiency and ease of use. Furthermore, when used correctly, an ABD will provide any belayer with increased security and a margin of error that cannot be duplicated by a tuber device. The modern outdoor climber should acquire and learn to use both tools.

Common ABDs: Petzl GRIGRI 2 and Trango Cinch.

Bringing it all together: examples of a climbing kit for a day of toproping at the crag.

Knots, Hitches, and Bends

In indoor settings climbers at least learn to tie the figure 8 follow-through, and they may even learn the figure 8 on a bight. An indoor facility, by design, usually does not require any additional knot craft. Outdoors, individuals must learn to use new kinds of knots and make application choices, selecting one knot, hitch, or bend over another. In this chapter, we will discuss the main tasks that climbers use knots, hitches, and bends (material joining knots) for;

Things to Understand about Knots, Hitches, and Bends for the Crag

- Knot terminology and parts
- Tying methods
- Effects on the climbing rope
- How much weaker the rope is after application (all knots, hitches, and bends decrease the load-bearing capacity of a rope) and why
- How much time tying takes
- After usage and loading, how much time untying takes

which are most common and effective for those tasks; and how to tie and use each within those common applications.

In an indoor facility, there are certain advantages for uniform ropework and knot-tying practices among all participants. It makes instruction and supervision easier and more efficient. As a result, climbers often learn that ropework is done a certain way, without alternatives or a need for decision making. Outdoors, these guidelines disappear, and so a climber will need to understand knots and hitches differently. The better informed a climber is in this area, the better choices about where, when, and why to use a particular knot or hitch can be made.

Definitions

Bend: a knot construction that joins the ends of rope, webbing, or cordage (aka joining knot).

Bight: a section of rope, webbing, or cordage that does not cross itself; also useful in knot or hitch construction.

Dressed: a knot, hitch, or bend is dressed when it is correctly tied without any unnecessary crosses or twists. A dressed knot is also set to eliminate any loose parts that could snag. Extra crosses or twists make your knot weaker! Dressed knots are easier to inspect, verify, and untie; they function better and are stronger! Dress and stress all knots (tighten and check)!!

Hitch: a construction made around something to hold its form.

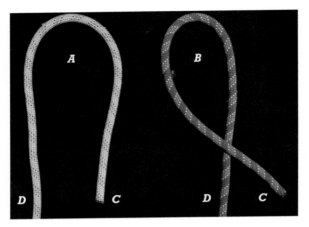

A. a bight (left) remains open

B. a loop (right) crosses itself

C. standing end

D. working End

Knot: a construction that always holds its form.

Loop: a section of rope, webbing, or cordage that crosses itself; these are useful in knot or hitch construction.

Running or working end: the part of the rope, webbing, or cordage that runs into more rope, webbing, or cordage to a climber or is used to tie a knot.

Standing end: an unused part or the end of a rope, webbing, or cordage.

Strengths of Common Knots and Hitches*

Knot or Hitch	Approximate Strength (%)
No knot	100
Figure 8 (retraced or bight)	75–80
Double bowline	70–75
Double overhand	65–70
Clove hitch	60–65
Double fisherman's	65–70
Rope through carabiner	79
Munter hitch, alpine clutch, and friction knots	Depends on the type of cordage used, its application, and the number of times the rope/ cordage crosses itself

* Based on use with a single dynamic kernmantle rope.

Connecting the End of the Rope to the Climber: Figure 8 Follow-Through

One task that will be familiar to all climbers is attaching the end of a rope to the climber. By far the most common knot used to accomplish this is the figure 8 follow-through.

Why do we use the figure 8 follow-through?

- The figure 8 follow-through reduces rope strength by only 20 percent (at most), so it is a very strong knot.

- Easy to inspect

- Widely accepted standard

The figure 8 follow-through should be dressed, with a 6-inch tail and no sizable gap between the knot and the harness.

The figure 8 follow-through, dressed, with a 6-inch tail and no sizable gap between the knot and the harness.

Connecting Rope to Carabiner: Figure 8 on a Bight or Clove Hitch

Climbers will often discover that they need to connect the rope to a carabiner. Sometimes we connect the climber to the rope with carabiners; sometimes we need to connect a climber to a ground anchor; sometimes we need to attach the rope to a master point. In each case, there are two obvious options: the figure 8 with a bight or the clove hitch. The strengths and weaknesses of those two options help us make the right choice.

The *figure 8 with a bight* offers all the same strength and recognizability as the figure 8 follow-through. Most commonly it is deployed when a rope is connected to something important such as an anchor component, where all users will want to be able to inspect and verify the integrity of the knot throughout its use. It is a natural progression to use this knot because of its familiar structure.

Figure 8 with a bight.

Clove hitch.

By contrast, the *clove hitch* is not as strong, and its behavior at high loads is more variable. In one circumstance, it may slip at loads well beneath the material strength of the rope. In another, it may bite down and snap the rope, much like the figure 8 with a bight under high loads. These forces are very rare in all of climbing and virtually nonexistent in toproping. But, unlike the figure 8 follow-through or figure 8 with a bight, the clove hitch is very easy to tie and untie. Not only that, but it can be adjusted quickly, and this adjustment can happen without untying the hitch. As a result, the clove hitch is usually used to secure smaller loads, like a static body weight, and when the only person who needs to supervise or inspect the integrity of the hitch is the person using it.

Connecting the Rope to an Object: Bowline

When tying a rope around a tree or a boulder, one of the strongest and most efficient options is the bowline. A climber can take the rope, circumnavigate the object, and tie the bowline wherever they end up. But the bowline can behave erratically if the tail of the knot is not long enough: Very short tails can slip out of the knot at high loads. As a result, it is a standard and advisable practice to tie a backup knot when using a bowline. When a backup knot is applied, bowlines tend to behave in more predictable ways.

A bowline with double overhand backup utilized as an attachment to a tree.

Creating an Anchor Master Point: Big Honking Knot (BHK)

It is desirable to create a bight knot that has more than one strand of material within its loop. Anchor systems, for example, strive to achieve this kind of material redundancy at their connection point. The BHK is one of the easiest ways to accomplish this task. Essentially this knot is a bighted bight tied in an overhand configuration.

Connecting a Sling to the Harness: The Girth Hitch and the Basket

Climbers routinely need to use a nylon sling to connect themselves to an anchor. When doing so, there are two common options: A shoulder-length or

BHK, aka monster knot, in action.

double-length sling can be girth hitched to the harness, or the double-length sling can be basketed. The girth hitch is a tricky and unpredictable contortion of any material, and it can drastically weaken a sling's strength. A quick overhand knot in a basketed sling creates a connection point that is comparable in redundancy and strength to any harness's belay loop. Given the option to do so, the basketed sling with a knot can be a very persuasive tethering method.

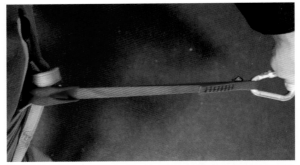

Girth hitch.

Basket hitch with an overhand knot.

Joining Two Rope Ends: The Double Fisherman's and the Flat Overhand

When joining two rope ends, climbers tend to default to two particular bends: the double fisherman's and the flat overhand. The *double fisherman's* is a strong and reliable way to join to rope ends of the same diameter, and it is commonly used to join two ropes that will never be untied, like an accessory cord loop or a cordellette. The *flat overhand,* by comparison, is not as

Double fisherman's.

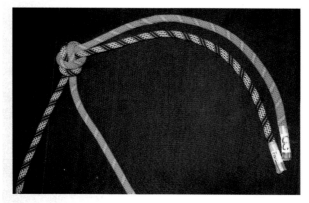

Flat overhand.

strong, can behave erratically at high loads, and must be tied with 10-12 inch tails to avoid catastrophic failures in high-load applications. But, unlike the *double fisherman's*, the *flat overhand* is fairly easy to tie and easy to untie, even after a high load. The flat overhand is most commonly used to join two ropes of similar diameter for rappelling.

Friction Hitches: The Prusik and the Autoblock

Friction hitches are typically tied with accessory cord or cordellette around a rope. They work by creating friction, which is dependent on the difference in diameters between the rope and the cord being attached. The greater this difference, the more potential friction and thus holding power.

Accessory cord loops are often used as backups for rappelling and lowering. These loops can be used to create the Prusik or an autoblock. The *Prusik* is somewhat tedious to tie and dress properly; if it is not properly dressed, it can be difficult to predict its holding power. But, when tied correctly, it is a reliable and strong friction hitch. The *autoblock,*

Prusik.

Autoblock.

by comparison, does not have the same holding power as the Prusik, but, the autoblock is much quicker to tie and untie than a Prusik. As a result, we tend to use the autoblock as a backup for lowering and rappelling, where the relative strength of the brake hand is all that the hitch needs to perform. The autoblock is more than adequate for these tasks, and is efficiently deployed and deconstructed. The Prusik is usually reserved for more vital applications in improvised rescue or rope ascension.

Outdoor Climbing Culture

The first visit to a climbing gym is probably as bewildering and awkward as any attempt to join a new community or learn a new sport, or the beginning of a long journey. One's first outdoor climbing experience is not much different for the novice venturing out from the gym. This process is longer and more difficult, but ultimately extremely rewarding. Appropriate guidance and mentorship must be sought; it's not just waiting at the door. An appropriate progression and learning curve can be dramatically different from one user to the next.

In this chapter, we will create a portrait of the climbing community based on the main categories of users that a novice climber is likely to encounter at any given crag on any given day.

Climbers are likely to encounter four main categories of climbers: a novice, a toproper, a lead climber, or a professional. It's important to start in the right place, know all the characters when they present themselves, and make a thoughtful and conscientious progression from one category to the next. Transitions can be disruptive and dangerous, if inappropriate or unprepared.

The Novice

While many of the skills that are mastered in a climbing gym have immediate use and context in an outdoor setting, there still is much to learn. Being receptive and humble, and having the right attitude and a curious personal responsibility are characteristics that will ultimately result in a faster matriculation to more advanced climbing skills.

Novices may not yet have all the tools needed to participate on their own. They may be sharing equipment with others, using rental equipment, or borrowing from a friend. They may not yet have adapted to the unique eccentricities of movement outdoors. They may not be familiar with the technical skills needed to go on outings by themselves, like anchoring, cleaning, and rappelling. They may not be prepared to deal with emergencies if and when they occur.

Thus novice users should be very careful about how they choose to go outside, when, and with whom. When novices presume to take other novices climbing, the overall deficits in experience and understanding can be dangerous and culturally destructive.

The Professional

One of the easiest and most logical ways to rapidly matriculate through technical and experiential skills is to work with a professional climbing instructor or guide. An instructor is capable of figuring out where a student's skills are currently, assessing their goals, designing a curriculum to take them where they want to go, and providing helpful support and remediation along the way. A professional is likely to provide current and definitive information, not hearsay, myth, or rumor. A professional can provide all the equipment a novice will need to learn comfortably. Also, the professional can give informed recommendations on what to purchase for this new climbing environment. Lastly, a professional is trained and prepared to deal with emergencies should they ever occur. First aid training and supplies, improvised rescue expertise, and liability insurance are just some of the ways a professional is prepared to take responsibility for the students in his or her care.

Professionals have undergone training and certification that distinguishes their instruction from informal mentorship between climbers. They are likely to be pillars in the local and regional climbing communities. AMGA Single Pitch Instructor (SPI) certification would be the minimum credential to look for from a professional.

The Toproper

Toproping is one of the first ways that outdoor climbers learn to use and enjoy a crag. Many outdoor climbers are perfectly happy and find a lifetime of satisfaction from toproping.

Because most indoor climbing involves toproping, it is one of the first ways that novices will learn to use an outdoor crag, but it would be foolish to assume that any indoor climber is ready to go toproping with their indoor experience alone. Topropers will need equipment to build anchors on top of the climb and on the ground. They need to know how to deal with small emergencies and how to keep themselves safe at all times: on top of the cliff, while climbing, and while moving around at the base of the crag. Helping an indoor climber transition from novice to toproper is one of the primary goals of this text.

The Lead Climber

Lead climbers have learned to use a protection system where they start at the bottom of the cliff with all their equipment, implement the protection system as they climb to the top of the climb, and finally create and use an anchor—all without injuring themselves or others. Many outdoor lead climbers discovered lead climbing in an indoor setting, so they are already familiar with the status and hierarchy that lead climbers possess. They have probably already experienced the exhilaration of managing lead fall consequences and possess the stamina needed to clip protection as one climbs, and the satisfaction of successfully leading a difficult route. Lead climbers have access to types of cliffs where toproping is not possible unless a lead climber puts a rope in place. It is considered good etiquette to allow lead climbing parties to enjoy the right-of-way on any given pitch or climb.

A Recommended Progression from One Category to the Next

The climbing gym can be a great training and reinforcing environment for an outdoor climber. A thoughtful and responsible progression to outdoor climbing might move along the following trajectory.

Novice Step 1: Climb in the Gym.

Learn to toprope belay with a plate/aperture/tube style device and a GriGri (ABD), learn the figure 8 follow-through, and learn how to move in vertical terrain. Have fun!

Novice Step 2: Engage with a Professional (hire a instructor or guide, or join a professional outdoor climbing outing).

Hire an AMGA–certified climbing instructor or guide to introduce a local crag and best practices. Learn Leave No Trace (LNT) practices and ethics. Learn outdoor movement. Learn what equipment brands, models, and sizes fit you best. Learn to belay and ground anchor outdoors. Learn to rappel. See a high standard of climbing technical skills in action.

Novice Step 3: Go Shopping. Purchase Gear.

Purchase your own climbing shoes, harness, helmet, belay devices with locking carabiners, chalk bag, backpack, and apparel for outdoor climbing, if you don't own them already.

Toproping Step 1: Go Climbing with an Informal Mentor or Professional.

Your informal mentor or professional instructor can teach you how to tie more knots, how to build anchors, how to clean anchors, how to safely navigate all parts of the cliff, and how to deal with emergencies. Go climbing with them until you can do all toprope setup and take down practices safely and efficiently.

Toproping Step 2: Go Shopping Again. Purchase More Gear.

Having learned to build anchors, you can make informed purchases of slings, cordellette, accessory cord loops, climbing ropes, and carabiners. You will need gear to go on your own outings.

Work outside with a mentor or climbing professional.

Toproping Step 3: Go Climbing with Equally Skilled People.

You've just learned to toprope independently, so enjoy yourself!! Visit lots of places and see what local climbing areas have to offer.

Lead Climbing Step 1: Learn to Lead in the Gym.

If you haven't already done so, learn to lead and belay (with tuber and GriGri) as a leader in the gym. The gym is a great place to hone the fitness needed for lead climbing, understand fall consequences, and learn to take falls. If you can't lead in a managed indoor setting, it is imprudent to try to learn to lead outdoors.

Lead Climbing Step 2: Learn to Lead Sport Climbs with an Informal Mentor or a Professional.

Learn all you can about sport climbing.

Lead Climbing Step 3: Learn to Lead Traditionally Protected Climbs with an Informal Mentor or a Professional.

Learn all you can about trad climbing.

Professional Instructor Step 1: Become an Experienced, Knowledgeable, and Well-Traveled Climber.

Build your climbing résumé. Go on a road trip—live the dream!

Professional Instructor Step 2: Seek AMGA Training and Certification.

Preparing for and obtaining a Climbing Wall Instructor (CWI) and/or Single Pitch Instructor (SPI) certifications are great first steps.

CHAPTER 9

Belaying

When climbing outdoors, belaying will not be that much different from indoors. The fundamental principles of belaying remain the same. Indoors, however, belaying is not always taught in terms of its fundamental principles. Typically, climbing wall instructors strive to teach belaying as efficiently as possible, to get people using the wall. But, in general, the things that were true indoors are also true outdoors.

A good toprope belayer never lets go with their brake hand and is focused on managing risk, in addition to these qualities:

- Keeps the climbing rope tight on the climber

- Catches a climber fall

- Safely and slowly lowers the climber

A tuber set up and ready to belay.

An effective toprope belayer using an ABD.

Belaying Differences: Indoor versus Outdoors

Indoor facilities do not always allow or necessitate any decision making in terms of belay method or device. Outdoor belayers need to be better informed and make more independent decisions from one climb to the next in order to maintain a proper belay and keep each other safe.

Fundamental Principles of Belaying

Historically, through all techniques, tools, and terrain, belaying has always had irreducible principles:

- A brake hand must always be on the rope.

- Any transitions or shuffling of the brake hand should happen in the braking plane (the plane below the device where maximum friction is employed).

- The belayer's hands, arms, and body should be comfortably and sustainably positioned throughout the belay cycle. Ergonomic—You are situated so belaying can be done for a long time.

- In the event of a fall, the break position is easily attained.

There are secondary considerations that all belayers should also account for:

- If the weight discrepancy between the climber and belayer is greater than 40 percent, backup belayers and ground anchors should be strongly considered.

- Because lowering is such a critical time in the belay cycle, two hands, backups, or the use of an ABD can increase the security of the belay system.

- The system should always be closed (see Chapter 10).

- The use of belay gloves can increase grip strength, decrease the likelihood of friction burns, and keep the belayer's hands clean.

- In an effective belay, no slack should be allowed in the rope system. A taut system can decrease the impact hazards associated with rope elongation.

An anchored belayer.

PBUS–The modern belay method standard

Pull: Pull the rope through the belay device.
Brake: Go to the brake position.
Under: Put your guide (non-brake) hand on the rope under the brake hand so that you can keep the brake hand on the rope!
Slide: Slide the brake hand closer to the belay device and reset for the next PBUS.

An example of an effective belay method
The PBUS: pull, brake, under, slide.

Sync the upward pull by the brake hand
with the downward pull of the non-brake hand.

EXAMPLES OF BACKUP BELAYS

Two Hand Brake Backup

- The guide hand slides the rope through a fixed brake hand.

- Make sure you allow enough slack between this backup and the primary belayer to create a "smiley face" with the rope. This allows the primary belay to efficiently belay while preventing excess and potentially dangerous slack in the system.

- Stay in the braking plane of the belay device and be prepared to pull down the rope to a full brake position.

Hip Belay

- The rope is placed around the hip and a slip–slap–slide hip belay is used. Slip the rope around your waist, slap above your brake hand and slide the brake hand back to the start position near a hip to repeat the process.

- Make sure you allow enough slack between this backup and the primary belayer to create a "smiley face" with the rope. This allows the primary belay to efficiently belay while preventing excess and potentially dangerous slack in the system.

- Be prepared to go into a brake position around your hip and down toward the ground.

Autoblock

- Tie the autoblock around the brake strand.

- Manage and tend it (so it does not grab when you do not want it to) as you lower (this is common in top belays).

Knots

- Tie knots, like an overhand on a bight, every 2m or so as slack is generated from the primary belay.

- Untie these knots when needed during the lowering of the climber back down.

*Backup Belays:
two hand brake
and knots.*

The fundamental principles of belaying and all secondary considerations allow enormous flexibility and decision making. It might help outdoor belayers to imagine the strongest, most secure, most universally applicable belay setup first and foremost. Then, as the terrain, the climbers, or the circumstances dictate, it may be appropriate to simplify that system.

In this system, the belayer and the climber are comparably sized. The belayer chooses to use a Gri-Gri. The belayer is ground anchored on the brake hand side with the climbing rope. The ground anchor, the belayer, and the climbing rope all form a straight line when tensioned—the ABC line where the rope between the bottom anchor, belayer, and climber are in a sensible and stable alignment. They will become straight under tension from a lower or fall, so it is important to set up this way so they cannot move to compromise the belay. There is also a backup belayer standing in the braking plane of the GriGri, who manages the rope stack and ties bight knots every 6 to 15 feet.

Belaying is at the core of climbing. Starting with a universally applicable system is a sound practice when moving outside. Deviating from such a system, should be an informed and deliberate decision. There should be a good reason why. It is in these decisions to deviate where consequences could be felt by the belay team inexperienced with belaying outdoors.

CHAPTER 10

Best Practices

When an indoor climber makes his or her first trip to the crag, there is a handful of common best practices to keep in mind, and learning these through informal mentorship and professional instructors is perhaps the best method. This chapter is designed to serve as a reference and a to-do list for the aspiring outdoor climber.

Communication and Double Checks

Many indoor climbers will be familiar with the climber's and belayer's verbal code or contract. This communication is recognizable as the ritual that inaugurates and continues through a climb. Outdoors, this communication is also vital, but it is even more important that climbers understand what needs to be confirmed and communicated and why a codified way of doing so is good safety mechanism:

- It cues a double check of the system.
- It provides an unambiguous understanding of when the climbing relationship will begin and end.
- It provides status updates about the climbing system and participants.

A climber who is far away, scared, tired, or soft-spoken can be hard to understand; that's why we need a codified and precise way of performing our communication ritual with a prearranged script that all parties know by heart, can recite in times of stress, and can execute without need for other verbiage. Here is good one:

The Belayer: Derek

The Climber: Susan

Act I, Scene One. The Contract

At the beginning of our scene, we find Derek and Susan. Susan is ready to climb, tied in with a figure 8 follow-through, helmet on, harness properly fitted, climbing shoes on, hands chalked, spirit psyched. Derek is situated in a comfortable and safe place, his helmet is on, his harness is properly fitted, the rope is stacked neatly behind his brake hand atop a rope bag, there is a knot in the end of the rope, his GriGri is connected to the rope correctly, and he has pulled the rope tight against Susan's body weight.

SUSAN: Am I on belay, Derek?

[Derek wishes to answer the question, so he visually inspects everything. So does Susan. They can see Susan's knot, her harness, and her helmet; the rope is tight and unencumbered or snagged; Derek's GriGri is rigged correctly and his carabiner is locked; the rope is stacked neatly at his feet; and the system is closed. Having visually inspected all of these things, Derek feels confident in his reply.]

DEREK: The belay is on, Susan.

SUSAN: I'm climbing, Derek.

DEREK: Climb on, Susan.

Act I, Scene Two. The Climb

Susan begins to climb. As she does, she may speak, or she may not. None of these words are vital. Derek may respond, or he may not. None of his responses are vital. When Susan wants slack, she says "Slack, Derek!" When she wants Derek to pull the rope as tight as possible she says, "Take, Derek!" Eventually, Susan reaches the top of the climb.

Susan: Take, Derek.

Derek: Gotcha, Susan.

Act I, Scene Three. The Lower

Susan leans back and puts her weight on the rope. She knows that nothing else can happen until she puts her weight on the rope, and she doesn't need to say anything else until then.

Susan: Ready to lower, Derek.

Derek: Lowering, Susan.

Derek lowers Susan to the ground. When she is safely planted, with firm footing, she no longer needs to be belayed. She is ready for Derek to stop belaying.

Act I, Scene Four. The Separation

Susan: Off belay, Derek.

Derek: Belay Off, Susan.

[Curtain]

Derek and Susan's script is a common one, and it can be easily imitated. Their ritual does all the things climbers need to do:

- The intentions and roles are clear.

- They double-check each other, head to toe.

- They precisely initiate and terminate the climbing.

Minimal and unambiguous verbiage makes it clear what is happening and when. Both climbers use each other's names to punctuate all vital communication, making it absolutely clear who is talking to whom.

You may see variations or modifications of the communication system outlined here. This is OK. Just be sure that your communication strategy accomplishes the following: clarity to all participants, concision (too many words are confusing), and double checks of the system and the participants.

There are a few other commands a climber may need to signal to the belayer:

- Climber: "Up rope, [name of belayer]." (That is, *Please pull in all the slack in the rope, but I still am climbing. I am not ready to be held or lowered.*)

- Anyone: "*Rock, rock, rock*!!" (That is, A falling object; take cover, do not look up. Yelled repeatedly until *any* object that has been dislodged has stopped.)

- Climber: "Watch me!" (That is, *It is a difficult move, I may fall.*)

Redundancy

It is important for all climbers to understand and apply the concept of redundancy to their anchors, belay systems, and most critical applications. An outdoor climber needs to understand when and how to apply the concept of redundancy.

One of the most supportive ways to help climbers understand the selective application of redundancy is to appreciate, from the beginning, that redundancy for its own sake is not really a climber's main goal. Security and safety are the goal; redundancy is just one of the ways that climbers create security.

Take a look at an average anchoring system, for example. Because an anchor is usually a critical life-saving system, anchor builders strive to create redundancy in the system. But the redundant anchor is routinely used to connect a single climbing rope to a climber. The single rope is clearly not redundant because there is nothing to back it up if it were to fail. Is the climber's risk management inconsistent? Climbers tend to ignore systemic and material redundancy when they can substitute supervision, management, or monolithic strength to create security.

Similarly, a single carabiner is often used to connect a belay system to a belayer. Like the climbing rope, the carabiner is more than strong enough to hold all potential loads in the belay system. Its locking mechanism can be inspected and supervised by the climber and the belayer.

Inspecting a carabiner's locking mechanism: the pinch test.

As a general best practice, it is important to create material and systemic redundancy when the following conditions exist:

- Combining materials and systems is needed to create an adequate load-bearing capacity for all potential loads.

- Constant supervision and management of the system is not possible.

- It is practical, efficient, and unobtrusive to do so. (Why wouldn't you make it redundant?!)

Backups for Belaying, Lowering, and Rappelling

If climbers consider the criteria above concerning redundancy, an obvious set of best practices when belaying and rappelling will emerge. Since it is almost always practical, efficient, and unobtrusive to have backups while belaying and rappelling, doing so is a best practice.

When belaying with a tuber/aperture device, for example, it is usually quick and efficient to enlist another climber to give a backup belay. It is usually quick and efficient to tie a friction hitch to backup a lower. These practices, when used individually or in combination, will give any belayer and climber a persuasive peace of mind as they climb.

When belaying with an ABD, it is interesting to imagine that the belayer's brake hand is providing a backup to the ABD's camming mechanism. If the inherent redundancy of that belay (when used correctly) is combined with backup knots, backup belayers, or friction hitches, the chances of a systemic or catastrophic failure are largely nullified.

When rappelling with a plate or tuber, a friction hitch backup is quick to deploy, easy to use, and quick to remove. Why not use one all the time?

Another easy way to give backup to a rappelling climber is to offer a fireman's belay; especially if there is another climber on the ground, why not? It is quick, efficient, and effective, and it greatly reduces the rappeller's likelihood of losing control of the rappel.

The rappel device is extended by connecting to a basket hitch with a knot that was created on the harness via a double-length sling. Tie a friction hitch with cordage (autoblock is used here) and connect it to belay loop with a locking carabiner. Test the functionality of the friction hitch prior to committing to it: Does it grab the rope and brake the rappel without slipping or colliding with the rappel device?

Tend the friction hitch and rappel away! If there is a situation that compromises your brake hand, you have backup.

Fireman's belay for a rappel: essentially an extra set of brake hands at the bottom of the crag.

Closing the System

It is an irreplaceable gesture of any climbing team to close the system. It should be done all day, every day! *Closing the system* means that both ends of a climbing rope are managed when the climbing rope is in use. One of the easiest and most convenient ways to close the system is to have the belayer tie into it with a figure

The climbing rope's other end is used to create a bottom anchor; the belay then connects to it.

8 follow-through. Not only does such a gesture close the system but the belayer is already tied in when her or his time to climb arrives. The climbing rope is an excellent ground anchoring tool. It can be used for this purpose, which also has the benefit of closing the system on the non-climbing end. And the literal connection between the climber and the belayer harkens

Closed systems have:

- prevented rappelling off the end of ropes
- prevented the end of a rope passing through a belay device when lowering
- helped manage risk in numerous other situations

to the mountaineering heritage shared by all climbing disciplines. Another way to close the system is to tie a bulky knot in any end of the rope that is not in use.

Too often, an unforeseeable circumstance occurs when lowering or rappelling. Climbers have lowered each other off the end of the rope, or rappellers have rappelled off open unknotted rope ends. It seems difficult to imagine—and careless—but even the most conscientious and experienced climbers have been severely injured or killed by such incidents. Unfortunately, through one twist of fate or another, climbs can be taller than we think they are, or the rope can be shorter. Parties who are in the habit of closing the system are less likely to lower each other or rappel off the ends of a climbing rope. A closed system can prevent this catastrophe.

Other Best Practices

Many climbers have learned to manage the risk involved from some climbing movements and actions from their indoor experiences. Here are few reminders and some unique aspects of being outside.

- Be careful about climbing too far left or right of your top anchor and incorporating a potential swing into a fall.

- At a crowded cliff, avoid climbing too close to or above another climber. Being too close or above can cause collisions in the event of a fall.

- Avoid touching, grabbing, and stepping up bolts, pitons, and fixed anchors. Poorly timed falls can injure digits.

- Be conservative and aware of ground hazards at the start of a climb. A fall near the ground and the resulting rope stretch will likely cause a climber to hit the ground (even with an excellent belay).

- Do not block a belayer's view of their climber (or distract him or her in any way), for example, by walking in front.

- Consolidate your stuff, leash your dog, and so on. (See Chapter 2.)

- If you are throwing a rope off a cliff, yell "rope" at least two times before throwing it. Consider lowering a rope down instead of throwing.

- If you hear the Rope command at the bottom of a cliff, move away and respond with "Clear"—if you are out of the way. If you are not out of the way, get out of the way!

- Do not leave your rope on a climb unattended. Use it or lose it!!

- Lead climbers get the right of way.

- Share! If you are on a popular climb for a long time and others want to climb it, move along and climb elsewhere.

Anchoring

In an indoor climbing environment, anchoring is rarely a skill with which climbers will need to be proficient. Outdoors, climbers not only will need to know how to build toprope anchors, but they will need to help their climbing team supervise the anchor throughout its usage. Additionally, climbers interacting with other climbing parties at any given crag will need to evaluate any anchor they did not build if an invitation to share ropes or anchors is offered.

Like many of the skills we have explored so far, anchoring is a widely variable and adaptable skill set. This entire book could easily focus on the subject. We'll narrow the focus of this chapter by concentrating on anchors that have comparably strong permanent components, like trees, boulders, and bolts. We'll focus on anchors where the direction of load applied by the climbing team is constant and uniform (unidirectional). We will also assume that the only anchors being built by a climber at this stage have easily accessible (with low risk) components.

Anchors consist of *components, attachments,* and the *master point.*

Components

Components in toproping are primarily bolts, trees, and large boulders. Some toproping areas require the use of removable protection, like spring-loaded camming devices (SLCDs) and stoppers, to create components, but those kinds of protection and anchors will not be the focus of this book.

Attachments

Attachment tools really come in two general varieties: long attachments and short attachments. Long attachments are most useful when components are big and far apart, like tree and boulders; 100 feet of 9mm static rope is usually just right. Short attachments are most useful when components are close together, like bolts. Double-length slings, cordellette, and an assortment of locking carabiners are effective and versatile short attachment tools.

Master Point

The master point is the load-bearing and redundant focal point of an anchor. It is where everything comes together, and all critical attachments occur.

BHK master point with two locking carabiners with opposite and opposed gates.

Fundamental Principles of Anchoring

Anchors should be simple, require minimal equipment, and be efficiently constructed and disassembled. The following anchor principles will be the most helpful.

Strong

An anchor should be strong enough to hold all potential loads that the climbing team can generate. Let's simplify and round off the mathematics by stipulating that the largest potential load a climber and a belayer could ever apply to a toprope anchor is 2,000 pounds.

If anchors are constructed that have twice the load-bearing capacity that any climbing team could ever generate—a 100 percent margin of error—most climbing teams can rest assured they will have an enjoyable and uneventful climbing experience.

The strength of an anchor is always calculated as a sum of the anchors parts. Two bolts may have up to 50kN of combined holding power, but the slings and carabiners that are clipped to the bolts may not have the same load bearing potential. As a result, the load bearing potential of anchor always hinges on the sum of the weakest parts of the anchor. When this sum exceeds 4,000 pounds, the strength of an anchor

Pitfalls to anchor strength:

- Weak or faulty attachment materials

- Weak or faulty components

- Catastrophic mistakes in knot tying or carabiner usage

should not be a concern. Be wary: A well-placed bolt may have a massive manufactured strength and high load-bearing potential; a poorly placed bolt does not. Slings may be manufactured to hold enormous loads, but damaged, old, or misused slings will not.

Redundant

Because it is difficult to inspect and supervise a toprope anchor all the time, redundancy is one of the most common ways to create security, reliability, and provide backup if part of the system proves to be unreliable. The redundancy of an anchor is evaluated by imagining the failure of any component or segment. Are there other components and attachments to back it up and ensure redundancy?

Remember, as climbers, we often forgo the concept of redundancy when monolithic strength can create security. Gigantic living trees that are perfectly positioned above a climb can commonly provide nonredundant, one-point anchors that are more than satisfactory.

No Extension

Most systems that create redundancy also negate any potential extensions and shock-loading in an anchor system. These are features anchor builders should strive to create. If there is an unexpected failure of any part of the anchor system, the master point should not extend toward the direction of load, thereby shock loading the remaining anchor parts or dropping a climber an unacceptable distance.

Intelligent Load Distribution

An anchor system and its master point should be perfectly positioned on the desired climb so that when the largest loads are applied to it, the attachment system distributes loads to the components as intended. For the toproping anchors we have specified, the load should be distributed intelligently to all the components.

Be intelligent with angles in the attachment system. For any load on an anchor system, the angles between the components and the master point can either distribute the load intelligently or drastically exaggerate the loads applied to the components. For a 1,000-pound load, angles would have the following effect:

Angle between two anchors (°)	Load distributed to each anchor (pounds)
20	500
40	540
80	700
90	750
120	1,000
160	2,900

The angles in the anchor system can be decreased by selecting different components or by using a longer attachment tool to lower the master point.

Efficient and Simple

Anchoring should be efficiently executed for climbing teams to enjoy an outing. If climbers are spending an inordinate amount of time building anchors, they may be ignoring the most obvious solutions to the problem. Experienced anchor builders should be able to construct and deploy a toprope anchor on a rock climb in less than 15 minutes.

Furthermore, if an anchor is unnecessarily complex, it is not only time-consuming, but it is difficult to inspect, evaluate, and supervise. There are also more potential places for error or misapplication of attachments.

Edgework

It won't matter how well an anchor is constructed if the anchor builder falls off the top of the cliff during the setup. In all setups, climbers will need to make careful decisions about how to stay safe while building an anchor, tossing the climbing rope down, and rigging to rappel. There are usually multiple options,

Be careful, stay low, use terrain barricade, stay back from edge.

Edgework	Security	Efficiency
Be careful, stay low, use terrain barricade, stay back from edge	Least secure	Highly efficient
Tether to component	More secure than nothing, but not as secure as tethering to a master point	Usually quick and easy
Tether to monolith	Highly secure	Usually quick and easy
Tether to master point	Fairly secure but can create potential shock loads and high impact forces if climber falls off the edge	Fairly efficient but sometimes impractical to set up
Prerigged rappel	Moderate security, but can create potential shock loads and high impact forces if climber falls off the edge	Sometimes highly efficient, but sometimes impractical to set up
Professional instructor tether	Highly secure	Advanced skills; least efficient unless practiced extensively

and no single option will always be most appropriate. Climbers have to select the technique that strikes a balance between security and efficiency.

Tethering to the master point: This anchor was built by attaching the ends of static rope to two components; the climber clipped a locking carabiner from the belay loop to a static line, moved closer to the edge, and then made a master point. The tether to the master point is a leapfrog transition, where a sling is first connected to the harness (basket hitch with a knot) and connected to the master point with a locking carabiner. The original carabiner from the belay loop to the rope is now removed, and progress toward the edge is continued.

Prerigged rappel: Set up anchor and backed-up rappel from secure terrain, then carefully maneuver anchor and rappeller over and onto the fall line.

Instructor tether: Professional instructors will often deploy a more versatile tethering method that allows them to use a GriGri and a high master point to extend over the cliff's edge. Such practices are effective and can be efficient, too!

Simple Toprope Anchors and Setup Procedures

With these anchor building principles in mind, climbing teams will discover slight variations on these three common themes: monolithic anchors, two-point fixed anchors, and natural component anchors.

Monolithic Anchors

When constructing an anchor on a monolithic feature, anchor builders should consider how the fundamental principles will be applied.

First: *strength*. If the anchor is going to be adequately strong, the monolithic feature needs to be solid enough and large enough to do all the work of the climbing system and provide an additional margin of error. Trees should be large (bigger than the climber and belayer's torsos combined at the trunk), living, and deeply rooted.

Monolith anchor. Component: huge tree; attachment: cordellette doubled up (basketed); master point: overhand on a bight.

Second: *redundancy and no extension*. A cordellette can be basketed around the tree near its base, and conjoined with a bight knot or BHK. This rigging doubles up the strands around the tree and prevents any extension should a strand of the cordellette break.

Third: *intelligent load distribution*. As long as the tree is perfectly positioned above the climb, it will assume 100 percent of the load of the climbing system. If the tree is not perfectly positioned, climbers will likely swing off their climb when they fall or when they lower. These swings can create impact hazards, rock fall, or abrade the climbing rope.

Lastly: *simple and efficient*. These kinds of anchors are incredibly simple and convenient. It is hard to imagine an easier alternative.

EVALUATION VIA NERDSS

No Extension: Yes.

Redundancy: All but the *huge* tree and the climbing rope. The cordellette is doubled up around the tree; it becomes two attachments.

Distribution: Single component gets all the system load; cordellette rigging shares the load.

Strength: Strong tree, rope, cordellette, and locking carabiners.

Simplicity: Very efficient and timely.

During the setup, anchor builders can keep themselves safe at the cliff's edge by connecting a double-length tether to the master point with a locking carabiner and rotating the anchor toward the climb, moving from a relatively safe to a relatively exposed position. Once exposed, the anchor builder can lower the climbing rope down, connecting the middle of the rope to the master point with two opposite and opposed locking carabiners. Retreat from the build can be either via backed-up rappel or reversing of the tethering steps. As always, sound judgment, risk management, and personal responsibility are required.

Two-Point Fixed Anchors

A pair of bolts usually results in one of the most common anchors in outdoor rock climbing. In this scenario, each end of a double-length sling is connected to each bolt. The saddle of the two connections is "ponytails" and used to tie a bight knot or BHK. Such an arrangement will most likely adhere to anchoring's fundamental principles, but the details are important and consequential. In terms of strength, this tactic will not be adequately strong if the bolts are too old or poorly placed, the carabiners are levered over the cliff's edge, the sling is damaged, or the BHK is not tied correctly. In terms of intelligent load distribution and no extension, the bolts will not share the load of the climbing system if the sling length between each bolt and the master point isn't exactly the same or the master point is not perfectly positioned above the climb. Nor will the bolts share the load if the angle between the BHK and the bolts is greater that 90 degrees. In

A common two-bolt fixed anchor.

Two-point anchor. Components: two good bolts; attachment: double-length sling (ponytailed); master point: overhand on a bight at saddle.

either case, one bolt will be doing most of the work, or the load to each bolt will be multiplied, or there will be potential shock loading of one bolt or the other.

EVALUATION VIA NERDSS

No Extension: Yes.

Redundancy: Yes.

Distribution: Shares the load.

Strength: Strong bolts, rope, sling, and carabiners.

Simplicity: Very efficient and timely.

During the setup, the anchor builder can stay safe by building the anchor in a reflexive manner; in other words, if the anchor is constructed in the opposite direction from the climb, the anchor builder won't be near the cliff's edge when it is constructed. After the anchor is complete, the instructor can connect to the master point with a double-length tether and locking carabiner. Lastly, the anchor can flip into position, like a hinging mousetrap, and the anchor builder will be securely fastened to the master point as the climbing rope is lowered into place.

In a similar manner, a pre-rigged quad (an appropriate soft good loop folded and tied at each end with overhand knots such that there are four stands of material in the middle) can be used for two bolt fixed anchors.

EVALUATION VIA NERDSS

No Extension: Minimal.

Redundancy: Yes.

Distribution: Shares the load.

Strength: Strong bolts, rope, cordellette, and carabiners.

Simplicity: Very efficient and timely.

Two-point anchor. Components: two good bolts; attachment: cordellette, prerigged into a quad (folded in half with overhand on a bights tied about one-third of the way from each end); master point: clip two or three of the strands in the "pocket."

Natural Component Anchors

Sometimes, anchor builders will need to combine more than one tree or boulder to make a satisfactory anchor with the desired strength. In this case, 100 feet of 9mm static anchoring rope is an ideal tool. One end of the rope can easily be attached to any number of natural features with a bowline. A variety of methods (a second bowline, a bowline with a bight or figure 8 follow-through) will close a massive loop that should hang just over the cliff's edge. From this loop, a BHK can be tied, and that master point should be perfectly positioned above the climb. This anchor will not be adequately strong if the knots are not tied correctly, or if the natural components are too small

Natural component anchor. Components: one solid tree and one solid boulder; attachment: static rope; master point: BHK.

or untrustworthy. It will not distribute system loads intelligently if the BHK in not perfectly positioned, or if the angle between the BHK and the components is greater than 90 degrees.

To stay safe during the construction of this anchor, anchor builders can attach a locking carabiner or a GriGri to either leg of the attachment system. This connection will keep them from falling off the cliff's edge while they tie a BHK.

EVALUATION VIA NERDSS

No Extension: Yes.

Redundancy: Yes.

Distribution: Shares the load.

Strength: Strong natural components, ropes, and carabiners.

Simplicity: Moderate; 15-minute construction is possible with practice!

Ground Anchors

A ground anchor, like any other anchor, should adhere to the fundamental principles of anchoring. The biggest difference between a ground anchor and an anchor at the top of the climb, however, is that a ground anchor will never need to be as strong as a toprope anchor. Ground anchors should

- have a master point at the end;
- be positioned on the belayer's brake hand side;
- be below or out of the way of the belay (no twists or crosses);

- be tight to the belayer and in line with expected forces, with no slack—anchor, belayer, and climber's forces, which will come from the top anchor's master point—should all be in a line: ABC line.

Various bottom anchors.

CHAPTER 12

Rappelling

Rappelling is a tool and a technique that is rarely practiced or rehearsed indoors. Outdoors, however, it is commonly used when setting up climbs, when cleaning anchors, or as a means of accessing the base of a cliff. No matter the application, all climbers should know how to descend a rope under their own control. Outdoor climbers will also need to know how to use this technique effectively, safely, and efficiently. This chapter will explore rappelling by first discussing the anchor, then the rigging, and lastly reviewing best practices to close the system and the use of a backup.

The Anchor

When a climber rappels down a rope, they either intend to pull the rope down from above when they reach the bottom (retrievable), or they wish to leave the rope in place (fixed). Two kinds of anchoring result from these two possibilities. If a climber wishes to pull the rope down when the rappelling is completed, it must run free and clear through an anchor, much like a toprope. So naturally, all the principles of anchoring should apply to the point(s) where the rope is connected to the top of the cliff. It must be strong, redundant, distribute load intelligently, and so on (NERDSS). If the rappel rope is to be left in place, the load-bearing properties of the anchor should also be

A messy and dubious rappel anchor: Make sure your rappel anchors or fixed lines follow NERDSS.

consistent (NERDSS), but a fixed line does not need to pull smoothly through the anchor like a toprope. As long as the rope is attached to something strong and all the connections are secure, fixed line rappelling does not require that many anchoring tools.

Some typical contexts of *retrievable rappelling*:

- After cleaning a fixed anchor
- After setting a toprope anchor
- To access the cliff base

Some typical contexts of *fixed rappelling*:

- To practice rappelling
- To rig a tether for edgework
- To access the cliff base

The Rigging

If a climber is rappelling down a fixed line, the ABD is an obvious choice for the rigging. It provides a smooth rappel, it does not require a secondary backup or fireman's belay, and it also can be used as an ascension tool if necessary.

ABD Rappelling Tips

- Use as if you are lowering a climber. When rappelling with an ABD, you are lowering yourself.

- Be gentle with the lever.

- Keep a brake hand on at all times.

- If you desire or need to go hands-free, you can tie a catastrophe knot (e.g., overhand on a bight) in the brake strand close to the device.

ABD rappel with a catastrophe knot to go hands-free.

Extended and backed-up rappel.

Tips for Rappelling

- Proper body position consists of:
    - Feet flat against the rock
    - Bent waist and straight legs (L-shaped body position)
    - Legs spread apart
    - Torso straight and parallel to the rock.
- Remove jewelry and tie back loose clothing or hair.
- Maintain a manageable speed.
- Limited lateral movement: Stay directly on the fall line, just like you're being lowered.
- Proper hand position: Keep the brake hand away from the device; avoid pinches!
- Grip: Have a solid grip on the brake but relax a bit and let the rope slowly move through.

If the rope is to be retrieved once the climber descends, a plate or tuber device is a logical choice. If the rappeller does not maintain an adequate brake at all times, it can be very dangerous. So, rappelling with a plate or tuber requires an adequate backup. One way to accomplish this backup is by using a fireman's belay. (See Chapter 10.)

If a fireman's belay is not available, it is common to use a friction hitch as a backup for a rappel. However, it is critical that the distance between the plate or tuber and the friction hitch be adequate to halt the progress of the rope if the rappeller loses control of the brake strand. As a result, it is common and advisable to extend the rappel device away from the rappeller's harness with a knotted basket hitch or other acceptable method. Then a friction hitch can be attached to the belay loop.

Lastly, it is wise to put knots into the ends of the rope. Rappels can be longer than anticipated, or ropes can be shorter. Putting a tight overhand with a bight into the end of the rope will keep a rappeller from gliding right off the ends of the rope.

In many instances there will be no partner to exchange communication and checks with; these cues and extra risk-management eyes will simply not be present. With due diligence, check everything before entering into harms way! Create a systemic approach that works for you and ensures you examine everything!

Rappelling Checklist

- Is the rope connected to an anchor that adheres to the fundamental principles of anchoring (NERDSS)?

- Is the rope end(s) touching the ground and knotted?

- For a fixed line, is the ABD loaded correctly?

- For a retrievable rappel, is the middle of the rope in the anchor? Do both ends touch the ground?

- For a retrievable rappel, are both strands of rope running through adjacent slots of the plate or tuber? Are they both clipped into the carabiner?

- Are all the carabiners vertically loaded and locked?

- Are the harness and helmet on properly?

- Are there adequate backups: a GriGri on a fixed line, an extended plate or tuber with a friction hitch backup attached to the belay loop, or a plate or tuber with a fireman's belay?

- Is the system closed? Are there knots in both ends of the rope?

- Double-check all aspects of the anchor and rigging before moving toward the cliff edge and rappelling.

CHAPTER 13

Emergency Preparedness

At a climbing gym, no one every really needs to worry about emergency preparedness. The staff is usually trained to deal with small issues, there is always access to an emergency response system, and urban response times for rescue personnel are usually quite fast. Outdoors, on the other hand, climbers need to be better prepared to deal with all incidents, both modest and severe. First aid training and supplies, communication devices, and improvised rescue skills are necessities that are easily neglected—until there is an accident, and suddenly climbers must scramble to help each other. The right tools, preparedness, and training help everyone achieve a greater sense of security, knowing that the climbers around them are prepared for an emergency.

First Aid Training and Supplies

At a minimum, all outdoor rock climbers should take a basic first aid and cardiopulmonary resuscitation (CPR) class. Help is often so far away that fairly modest injuries are prone to infection. Simple fractures and sprains can be aggravated by hikes and descents. Illnesses that would not be life-threatening become dire emergencies without immediate access to lifesaving drugs and medications. For these reasons, many climbers and most professional climbing instructors and guides maintain

- Leave plans and trip details with a family member or friend.

- Plan approaches and retreats (carry maps, guidebooks, etc.).

- Have emergency numbers, nearest help location or phone number, and hospital directions.

- Be aware of local hazards: bugs, poisonous plants, animals, and other site/environmental concerns.

a Wilderness First Responder level of first aid training and a professional rescuer level of CPR.

Whatever level of training an individual has achieved, it should be complemented with a corresponding first aid kit. Its contents should be in good condition, organized, and not expired. There are numerous sources to determine the contents. Your supplies should be researched and specific to the climbing site.

Communication

Outdoor climbers must be prepared to call for help. Here are some considerations for communication:

- Reliable cell phone coverage: Will I have to move to get it?

- Spare battery and recharging.

- Satellite telephones, communicators, and/or radios.

- What are the professionals using?

- Has the selected system been tested in the terrain?

Improvised Rescue Skills

This text cannot possibly cover the gamut of improvised rescue techniques in technical rock climbing.
The best way to learn a more comprehensive selection of these skills is to hire a professional climbing
instructor and work through a scenario-based curriculum. But there are a couple techniques that will be
imminently useful to any climber, on any cliff, in any
scenario.

Fixed line ascension with an ABD, friction hitch, and a double-length sling

Climbers should learn to climb a rope using some
basic ascension tools that they are already carrying. A
GRIGRI 2 for example, due to the engagement of its
camming mechanism, can be used as a progress cap-
ture for rope ascension. A Prusik and a double-length
sling can be used as an ascender and an etrier (step).
Together, the three tools will allow rescuers to ascend
a climbing rope.

Process for Ascending with an ABD:

- Slide a friction hitch runner combo up the
  rope and stand on it (sling).

- Pull rope through the ABD and sit on it (the
  sit).

- Repeat the stand and sit maneuvers for
  continued upward progress.

- Tie backup knots in the brake strand
  (overhand on a bight) every 2m or so.

Ascending in action.

To descend with an ABD:

- Tie a new backup.

- Remove the friction hitch and runner and rappel with ABD or GriGri.

- Maintain a presence on the brake strand and untie the backup knots as you move down.

Hands-Free at a Belay

Climbers should learn to tie a mule knot when using a tuber or plate. The knot allows the belayer to go hands-free. Going hands-free in and of itself may not solve many emergencies at the crag, but both hands might be needed to render first aid, make a cell-phone call, or assist another rescuer.

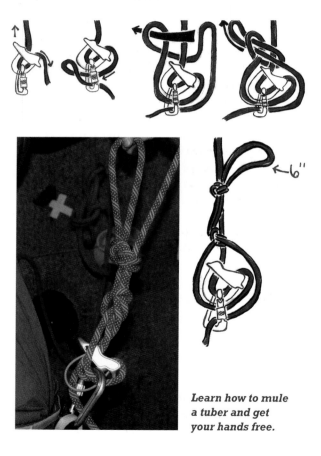

Learn how to mule a tuber and get your hands free.

Conclusion

Hopefully there is a solid to-do list in an aspiring outdoor climber's mind. Those first outings can be some of the most rewarding and formative climbing experiences in life. They can also be some of the most destructive experiences to the individual, the environment, and the community. Of course, as we have discussed, that need not be the case. Taking personal responsibility, accepting one's learning curve, acquiring new skills and experiences within an appropriate progression, and being prepared to deal with all the realities of outdoor climbing will ultimately spell the difference between a good experience and a bad one.

Every chapter of this book reinforces the action plan that we suggested in Chapter 8:

Step One: Take personal responsibility for what you know and what you don't know yet. Indoor climbing provides valuable experience, but there is much more to learn.

Step Two: Do your homework. Learn all about the crags you want to visit, the rock, the first ascents, the flora and fauna, the landowners, the routes, the anchors, and the local climbing coalition and its leadership. Understand where your climbing destination is, what it is, and who it is (does the cliff have a particular personality). These days, you can do all of that with a smartphone in less than an hour.

Step Three: Figure out where you fit into the climbing community and its culture. Hire an AMGA-certified guide to introduce you to the crag, the characters, and the equipment. With these experiences, you'll have a good idea about where you want to go next.

Step Four: Learn and grow. Don't be in such a hurry to arrive at a destination. Instead, understand the essential truth that all climbers' relish: There is no arrival, there is no destination; the journey is the whole point. That should apply to learning skills just as much as the Yosemite Decimal System. So hire an instructor and find a mentor, and when you have learned all the things in this book, go climbing with others of a similar skill set. Don't be in hurry to be a mentor if you are not ready for that level of responsibility.

Step Five: Repeat. Use this same progression every time you venture into a new aspect of the sport, like lead climbing, traditional climbing, multipitch, professional instruction, or mentoring others.

Have fun out there, and be careful.

About the Authors

Nate Fitch is a faculty member in the renowned Outdoor Education Department at the University of New Hampshire specializing in climbing courses/programming, and is the director of the Gass Climbing Center. He is an AMGA-certified single pitch instructor and apprentice rock guide who is also active in providing AMGA instructor programs in the climbing wall and single pitch disciplines. He lives with his wife and two kids in Durham, New Hampshire.

Ron Funderburke is an AMGA-certified rock guide. He is also a senior guide with Fox Mountain Guides and an AMGA SPI discipline coordinator.